Born Curious

Born Curious

New Perspectives in Educational Theory

R. A. Hodgkin
Department of Educational Studies
University of Oxford

JOHN WILEY & SONS
London · New York · Sydney · Toronto

Copyright © 1976 by John Wiley & Sons, Ltd

Library of Congress Cataloging in Publication Data:

Hodgkin, Robin A
  Born Curious

  Includes index.
    1. Learning, Psychology of. 2. Curiosity.
1. Title.
LB1051.H55   370.15′2   75–16340
ISBN 0 471 40220 6

Photosetting by Thomson Press (India) Limited, New Delhi and printed in
Great Britain by Pitman Press Ltd., Bath, Avon.

Preface

The approach to theory explored here starts from the view that an infant, or any other learner, is essentially active and questioning. This leads to a rejection of the idea of knowledge as facts and of any static notion of an 'educated man'. Despite Piaget, despite his successors and his critics and despite much good practice stemming from his ideas, the static view still lingers and is reflected in widespread instrumental assumptions about education, in the split between theory and practice which is evident in teacher training institutions and in our complacent philosophy of education.

I have had the good fortune to work in Africa and in England, in secondary schools, in teacher training and in curriculum development institutions where there was almost always a spirit of innovation and of experiment and recently it has been both a stimulus and a pleasure to work with experienced teachers who come to Oxford for a year's advanced study. In writing this book I have been assisted by many of these and indeed the book is partly written with such teachers in mind, experienced professionals who want to re-think their practices and their assumptions. A wider perspective has also been in my mind, for in many parts of the world teachers need to think afresh about the whole process of schooling and learning and to realize that it could become an exploratory and creative part of a self-renewing culture.

Educational theory has suffered from being kept in three isolated bottles marked philosophy, sociology and psychology. It needs mixing and shaking if a more interesting brew is to be made. Here I have done a little mixing. A certain number of speculations have resulted as well as by-products and problematic residues. Many of the footnotes, for example, are meant to be followed up in discussion and in further reading. Some statements in these, and in the text, are undoubtedly controversial. But teachers need controversy. Hackneyed references to 'motivation' and 'educational objectives' still float unchallenged around our seminars. Such phrases have become clichés which obscure real problems and delay the emergence of an adequate theory.

Some helpful critics have advised me to put in more diagrams and others to put in fewer. I hope readers who find the iconic mode, or my version of it, unhelpful, will not be put off. Similaraly with Chapters 9 and 10. these were written because one reader pressed me with the question 'What *is* a structure?' and I thought it right to attempt a provisional answer because the subject is so interesting. It must be confessed that this is a question which theorists in many disciplines touching on education—communication theory, linguistics and psychology—are actively probing. So our understanding is fragmentary and a comprehensive theory still eludes us. But there *is* a theory to be found.

University of Oxford
April 1975   R. A. HODGKIN

Acknowledgements

In writing this book I have been helped, directly and indirectly, by many people. Some have been generous in letting me use their ideas, others in reading and criticizing the manuscript. The following have been helpful in both ways and special thanks go to them: Professor J. S. Bruner and Mr. Rom Harré of Oxford University and Professor Marjorie Grene of Davis University. Mr. Robin Richardson has also given detailed help and criticism for which I am most grateful. And there have been others who have helped, especially certain D. Phil. and Advanced Course students at Oxford who have taken part in discussions round these themes. My wife, Elizabeth, has been constant in counsel and assistance and Adam Hodgkin has given useful criticism of two chapters. I have often, though not always, heeded my critics; Chapters 9 and 10, 12 and 13 have been written in a few months and have received less critical attention from friends. Mr. Paul Simmonds drew the diagrams and made them much more elegant and more intelligible than my originals. Christopher Hodgkin gave valuable help with proof correcting.

I also wish to thank the following for permission to quote copyright material: for the quotation from the *Times Literary Supplement*, Dr. T. G. R. Bower; for the examples of the Premack's sign language from *The Scientific American*, W. H. Freeman & Co.; for the quotation from Professor Peter's *Ethics and Education*, George Allen and Unwin Ltd.; from A. Schutz's *Collected Papers*, Martinus Nijhoff, The Hague; from Drs. Bannister and Mair, *The Evaluation of Personal Constructs*, Academic Press Inc. (London); Professor Marjorie Grene for an excerpt (from Chapter 3, 'F. J. J. Buytendijk', from *Approaches to a Philosophical Biology*, by Marjorie Grene, © 1965, 1966, 1967, 1968 by Marjorie Grene, Basic Books Inc., Publishers, New York); from Professors Bruner's and Waddington's papers in *Beyond Reductionism*, Mr. Arthur Koestler; from Robert W. White's 'Motivation Reconsidered', *The Psychological Review*, **66**, no. 5, 327 (Copyright 1959 by the American Psychological Association. Reprinted by permission); from Professor E. Laszlo, *The Systems View of the World*, George Braziller Inc.; from James Moffett's *Teaching the Universe of Discourse*, Houghton Mifflin, Boston; from Dr. John Shotter in *The Journal for the Explanation of Human Behaviour*, Basil Blackwell Ltd; from Professor J. M. Kennedy's *A Psychology of Picture Perception*, Jossey-Bass Inc.; the Republic of the Sudan for two pictures and a map; the Harvard University Press for extracts from Professor J. S. Bruner's *Toward a Theory of Instruction*, copyright 1968 Harvard University Press; Professor J. S. Bruner for a quotation and for the M. A. C. O. S. chart. There are a number of shorter quotations at chapter headings and elsewhere for which thanks are also due.

Contents

Part One

Space For a Theory

CHAPTER 1

Problematic Knowledge

Then I saw that ... the history of philosophy was no longer a body of facts which very, very learned men might know, [but] an open subject, an inexhaustible fountain of problems.

R. G. Collingwood[1]

We learn best as teachers; we teach best as learners. The effort to communicate strengthens knowledge and to be an authority is to know how to doubt. Many people have experienced this paradox, yet the deeper implications of the mutuality of teaching and learning are largely unexplored. Perhaps both sides of the process should be understood essentially as *arts* and therefore the method and theory which support them should derive from the uncertainties and extended skills of making and discovering, rather than from the conventional view of science as the establishment of certain knowledge and of education as passing it on. Indeed the whole educational endeavour needs to be seen as more perilous and problematic than has been customary. 'Problematic' here does not merely mean that education is puzzling, but rather that the essence of the process, from first to last, is to do with the control of doubt, with problems seen in the shadows, with the models that we make and share when we think we have found a solution, and with the underlying faith that there are more problems round the corner.

The theme of this book is that a new theory of education is in the process of emerging. Such a theory will eventually become explicit, but now it is implicit in much that is being done in imaginative and responsible teaching. Then why not let the yeast work? Why isolate the inconspicuous and powerful ferment and look at it? The answer is that teachers are not continuously engaged in a glorious creative enterprise. If we were, doubtless the best thing would be for us to press on till old age, martyrdom or television fame struck us down. But it is the nature of our calling to be sometimes deeply and actively immersed, while at other times we rest and shiver on the bank, wondering. We have to re-think and warm up from time to time, to re-align our ambitions and our priorities. As such re-thinking operations are partly joint endeavours, themselves involving questioning and criticism, we need a theoretical structure with which to work. The guidelines and common assumptions of such a structure, shared and continuously reshaped amongst colleagues, yet allowing for experiment and diversity, are necessary to any profession. The presence of such a shared 'philosophy', in the home-spun sense of the word, is more important to our morale, happiness and success than all the other paraphernalia of organizations, conferences, privileges and, even, pay.

WHY DIG OUT THEORY?

There is a fragmentary theory of education. Why should there not be a coherent one? Doubtless the practice of the art of education will always be more in evidence, more exciting and more eternally useful than its theory. Have we not all encountered extremely interesting and competent teachers as well as exceptionally lively schools? Do they work by luck or knack? They must, surely, embody principles that go deeper than those generally manifested in the literature of education. Good teachers are in fact often aware of the principles which guide their work and they are sometimes prepared to articulate these amongst colleagues; but they are also inclined to be suspicious of theorists and often hold to the view that principles are best learnt on the job. This is almost always true, but tacit knowledge of this kind is slowly acquired and slowly shared and if some of it is brought into consciousness as theory, the sharing can be quickened.[2]

Gilbert Ryle has summarized what ought to be a central educational principle in the phrase 'Efficient practice always precedes the theory of it.'[3] One should add a corollary, however, that inefficient trials usually precede efficient practice and therefore at *that* stage the presentation of theory may be positively harmful. We usually start an enterprise for reasons other than purely rational ones and these—our feelings, hopes, hunches, curiosities, habits and loyalties—ought to be of as much interest to educational theory as the reasons that can be treated logically.[4] But there is a dilemma here. If theory is only available for analysing actions retrospectively, what is its usefulness? This difficulty loses its hold when we stop regarding theory as a guide to one person's action and see it as something which is worked on by a group of people and which they use in criticizing and harmonizing their joint activity.

How is it that theories function in this social context? Firstly a theory contributes to a group's cohesion and effectiveness by allowing the members to envisage themselves *as* a group and thus to make limited plans and predictions. Secondly it encourages critical self-evaluation in the group and thereby increases the 'feedback' or flow of corrective information available. Thirdly it is of value in the design and evaluation of the tools and technologies with which a group develops and extends its powers. This is of special importance for teachers in over-developed countries who need to discriminate amongst the mass of tools and gadgets (pseudo-tools) which press upon them. And fourthly, to have theoretical knowledge helps us to pass it on—to extend the group in time so that younger or less experienced members can join. It must be said immediately, however, that *the theory of an art should not become the substance of instruction*. Theory in education, like grammar in language, should be not so much what we teach, but what a learner discovers. For the teacher theory can be the orderly system which enables him to arrange and present questions, experiences and rewards in an assimilable manner. Nevertheless as soon as a learner wants, or shows that he is ready for some portion of theory or grammar, he should have access to it and it will then strengthen the skill or concept he has just acquired.

THE METHOD OF ENQUIRY

'In framing metaphysical ideas', writes Whitehead, 'each ... notion should be given the widest extension of which it seems capable [for] only in this way can a true adjustment of ideas be explored.'[5] It is such an adjustment of ideas that is attempted here, an attempt to speak rationally but to stretch our framework so as to include actions and feelings on which reason rests. There will only be a little that is new, but the bringing together of a few old or contemporary things in unfamiliar proximity may lead to unusual questions being asked and, possibly, to changes of perspective. Sometimes it may do no more than confirm the good practice the reader already knows.

Four strands of enquiry will be followed:

1. We will take very seriously the currently developing view that new-born children have strongly patterned, innate yet flexible competence and that one aspect of this is a power to frame pre-verbal hypotheses and questions (Chapter 2).
2. We will try to see the phenomena of the learning process, both as they appear in the relative clarity of hindsight *and* as they appear in the relative obscurity of foresight. Because the development of such two-way vision in teachers is not helped by the fashionable analytic philosophy of education we will criticize this and will then suggest a possible alternative perspective. (Chapters 3, 4 and 5).
3. We will try to explore part of the interdisciplinary ground common to the sciences which bear on education such as ethology, linguistics and information theory, believing that the relevance of these to the work of teachers has not been given enough consideration. Chapters 6 and 7 examine the nature of play and competence and these are taken as fundamental elements in any theory of education. In this field, more even than in the others, there are methodological difficulties and the ideas that will be put forward are often speculative. Nevertheless, educational theory is almost certain to develop in interdisciplinary ways and so these speculations are intended as a push in that direction.
4. As far as possible our theoretical and metaphysical flights will be anchored in the *things and persons* of education. For example, the speculations about play and skill are also about toys and tools (Chapter 8). In the third part of the book an attempt will be made to integrate theories about instructional procedures of teachers and the cycle of heuristic activity with which children respond.

A necessary limitation of this book is that it scarcely touches the enormously important social field—how children and adults interact in large groups.

There is a great deal of thought and experiment going on in regard to this at the moment and it is probable that in the coming years important theoretical advances will be made. Teachers will need to know much more about the general theory of systems, about how language, non-verbal communication, art and ritual play a part in the patterning of educational communities. In the rest of this book the centre of our interest will be a triangle—the first and second elements of which are contained in that basic dyad of all education—mother/infant, adult/child, craftsman/apprentice, teacher/taught, and the third is—THINGS, those essential bits of informative matter which are shuttled to and fro across the gap between teacher and learner. We also take a tentative look at what systems theory and structuralism may offer to the educational theorist. In the model-building that is attempted no general theory of education will be articulated. Nevertheless there are some theoretical elements which appear to fit together in a promising way and others which nearly do.

We will start, then, with the new-born child and see how, even in its first few weeks, it is finding the world full of strange things which it sees and reacts to as problems.

NOTES

1. *Autobiography* (O.U.P., 1939), p. 75.
2. For a further and extended discussion of the idea of how 'tacit knowledge', shared unconsciously by people, can contribute to group action and group commitment, see Michael Polanyi's *Personal Knowledge* (Routledge and Kegan Paul, London 1958), especially the first five chapters. One of the central ideas, which Polanyi explores in many contexts, is that 'we know more than we can tell'. This is a book to which I am particularly indebted—hence a grateful acknowledgment in the title of my last chapter.
3. *The Concept of Mind* (Hutchinson, London, 1949), p. 30. See also M. R. Ayers, who takes issue with Ryle on the matter of *trying* ('inefficient trials'), *Refutation of Determinism* (Methuen, London, 1968), pp. 138–144.
4. 'The idea that people decide to adopt their moral principles seems to me a myth, a psychological shadow thrown by logical distinction.' Bernard Williams, 'Morality and the Emotions' in *Problems of the Self* (C.U.P., 1973), p. 227.
5. *Adventure of Ideas* (C.U.P., 1942), p. 305.

CHAPTER 2

Questions

It is nothing short of a miracle that the modern methods of instruction
have not entirely strangled the holy curiosity of enquiry.

Einstein[1]

Children often seem to perform miracles in overcoming the obstacles we
place in their way. But Einstein's *cri de coeur* is being given added force by
recent discoveries about the very high level of mental ability and curiosity
which children show at birth. It certainly appears that a good deal of what we
give them in the name of education delays their mental development. Delay,
however, may be as important as stimulus, just as giving free play may be as
important as providing structure; nevertheless if we are to understand education we need to have a clearer idea of how such complementary elements work
throughout the whole of childhood.

It now looks as though babies can formulate questions of a kind as soon as
they are born. They have the brain power to do this but have not acquired the
skill to manifest their 'doubts and hypothesis'. That this power exists was
shown vividly by experiments carried out in recent years by T. G. R. Bower in
Edinburgh. I shall quote an account of his at some length which not only
illustrates the discovery of unexpected powers in infants, but also introduces
an important idea about motivation—that the concept of motivation itself
may be largely a result of laboratory conditions or other extremely regulated
environments and has little relevance to free behaviour. Perhaps one should
preface Bower's account by saying that as far as the film records show the
infants who took part seemed to benefit from these experiments. Certainly
Professor Bruner's similar investigations, with slightly older children, are
conducted in an atmosphere of manifest enjoyment, in which the children
alternately smile, concentrate and then come back for more.

The following is Bower's account of a surprising discovery:

> In the first few days of life one can demonstrate learning of a very high
> order. [New born] infants can learn not one but a pair of response-reward
> contingencies, requiring two different responses signalled by two different
> stimuli. Thus a three-day old infant can learn to turn his head to the left
> to obtain reward, when a bell sounds, and to the right when a buzzer
> sounds. He can learn the bell-left, buzzer-right discrimination in a few
> minutes. Having learned it he can learn to reverse the discrimination

if the experimenter reverses the contingencies, to go bell-right, buzzer-left, again very rapidly. The learning displayed here is possibly of a higher order than is ever displayed by an infra-human. Why then is it so difficult to demonstrate learning in somewhat older infants?

Bower then describes how experimental psychologists used great ingenuity in designing exciting visual presentations with which to 'motivate' infants but they came to the conclusion that a simple flashing light is as effective as any of these elaborate alternatives. He then suggests that 'If the motivational effect is independent of the nature of the presentation, it follows that something else must be the source of motivation.' He then continues:

The something else, it now seems, is problem solving for its own sake. Infants perform in learning situations for no other reward than that they obtain from solving the problem posed by the situation. Attribution to infants of a thirst for learning for its own sake may seem an implausible step. However, there are a number of experiments which make the conclusion seem to be inescapable.

Consider an infant in a situation in which he can turn on a light by turning his head to the left. Most infants of two to three months will succeed in turning on the light several times within a quite short time. Their rate of leftward head-turning will then drop back to a level which is insufficient to serve as a criterion of learning. The rate will not pick up again so long as the left-turn-light-on contingency is operative. Suppose the experimenter changes the contingency to right-turn-light-on. Sooner or later the infant will make a left turn and the light will not go on. We then see a burst of leftward head-turns, followed by detection of the right-turn-light-on contingency, as shown by a brief, high rate of right head-turns, which will then subside. That rate, too, will stay low if the contingency is unchanged.

If, however, the contingency is changed again to a left-turn followed by right-turn to switch the light on, the rate of right-turning will increase after the first trial on which the light does not go on, the rate of left-rurning will also increase, and finally the infant will produce a left-turn followed by a right-turn and switch the light on. After a brief burst of left-rights the rate will subside, until the contingency is changed. The change produces a burst of activity, ending when the correct combination of movements is discovered. Infants have been brought to master quite complex series of movements, such as right-right-left-left, in such procedures. Every time the contingency is changed the activity rate goes up.

Examination of the behaviour shows that the activity is not random. The infants seems to be testing hypotheses, trying out sequences of movement to discover which one operates at the moment. It thus seems that the pleasures of problem-solving are sufficient to motivate behavioural and mental activity in these young infants. If a learning situation is interactive, the infant will demonstrate that he can learn: if it is not, and his only motive is the prospect of reward, then the infant will not demonstrate that he can learn.

Perhaps the most shocking thing about results like these is the remarkable capacity displayed by the infant subjects. Problem-solving, hypothesis-testing, learning for its own sake, are not phrases that we associate with infants. Indeed, experiments like these, which were originally undertaken to prove that infants begin life with few capacities, have in fact shown the reverse; learning of such a high order is only possible if other complex capacities are already present.[2]

It is shocking too how little we know about the nature of this questioning activity. At present a good deal of research is going on into the extent of this early hypothesis-making in children, though some authorities question Bower's more emphatic assertions.[3] I think we may expect that specifically educational investigations will be made along these lines especially in regard to the later developmental stages of children and to the extreme diversity and long-term effect of teachers' questions. In the education of teachers too one wonders why such a central question in education as *What is a question?* has not been given more attention. Here we shall have to be content with two short excursions, first a glance at primitive animal questioning and then we shall briefly survey the problematic, question-generating frontiers which, at any particular time, circumscribe all knowledge. The basic question about questions, however, will remain with us, asked, but only partially answered, throughout the book.

WHAT IS A QUESTION?

What Bower did was to pose questions to a very young infant, that is to say, he constructed a situation in which there was an anomaly. Now every oddity implies a background of 'normality'. You cannot have a question without a structure to which it belongs and from which, in some way, the question stands out. Anticipating subsequent discussion, it may be well to add that you cannot conceive a structure without a system in which it operates and within which it can be defined (See Chapters 9 and 10).

Throughout this book the theme will recur that education is to do with questions, not just asking them but, rather, creating questionable situations or appropriate constructions of linguistic or sensory material (e.g. visual aids) in which questions can be discerned by a learner. A question in essence is rather like a loose hook in wire netting. It is a break in the pattern of one structured system where another system—yours or mine for example—can link up. This is well illustrated at a simple level by recent attempts to teach chimpanzees to use language and, even, to ask questions.

David and Ann Premack successfully taught a simple sign language to a chimpanzee, Sarah. They used some 130 shaped and coloured plastic tokens of which Sarah gained considerable mastery. In describing their conversations

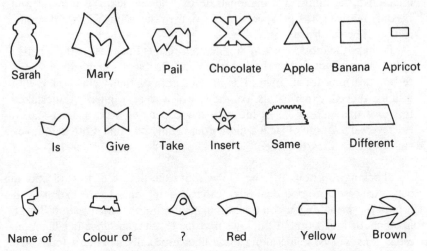

Figure 1. Examples of sign language for chimpanzees. (From Ann Premack and David Premack, *Teaching Language to an Ape*. Copyright ©1972 by Scientific American, Inc. All rights reserved)

with their pupil they bring out the essential nature of all questions when they say:

> Any construction is potentially a question. From the viewpoint of structural linguistics any construction where one or more elements are deleted is a question. ... Interrogation can be taught by removing an element from a familiar situation in the animal's world or by removing the element from a language that maps the animal's world.[4]

This account of what a question is may not go to the deep root of the matter but it does show up two essential attributes of questions to which we shall recur. Firstly a question implies recognition of some pattern *and* 'something missing' from it. Secondly it shows the asymmetry of questions. The Premacks and Bower set up a potentially linear construction of happenings, then they created in it a break, like a 'Y' fork on a road, and faced their 'pupil' with this option. The experimenter sees much of the surrounding structure; the pupil or discoverer usually sees little of it—but he does see the anomaly. Not only does each one see the elements of the problem differently but, as we shall see later, their emotional mood in facing it is likely to be in marked contrast. The 'instructor' usually regards a problem coolly and analytically; the discoverer, not unnaturally, faces it in a perplexed and more emotionally charged way. This is not an empirical observation but a deduction from general experience.

This asymmetry of problems is evident, both in time and in the vertical hierarchy of learner and teacher. The more you are 'under' and 'before' a problem in time, the more you are likely to face it with feelings, of fear, expected pleasure, curiosity or aggression; the more you can transcend and get above the problem and see it in the past, so you come to a position where you can distinguish its components, where you accept it and, if you wish, analyse it along lines of reason and causation.

THE FRONTIER

The rightness or wrongness of a question depends, in a primary sense, on the structure to which it applies: is there a pattern to which our doubts refer? In an important secondary sense 'rightness' depends also on the state of the person who may encounter the question. If I ask a physicist, 'What is gravity?' this may be a right question in terms of our combined knowledge and ignorance. I am aware of a structure of scientific knowledge which is certainly full of problems in the vicinity of 'gravity'. Gravity puzzles me and I guess it puzzles my physicist friend too, though in a more complex way. But if I were to ask a six-year-old child, 'What is gravity?' it would be a wrong question in the second sense—wrong educationally—because I ought to know that children at that age do not have the concepts to handle such a question.[5] Answering a 'yes or no' question admits of no degrees; understanding one admits of many and teachers should be more concerned with the degrees of understanding than with giving answers.

We need here to distinguish three horizons or frontiers between which the degrees of a teacher's questioning are stretched—his pupil's frontier, his own and a wider cultural frontier. Everybody sometimes works near his own frontier of knowledge, which I shall designate by a small f. On one side of it are well-tried skills, explanations and conceptual patterns which offer possibilities of control and articulation of relatively clear operations; but beyond it lie conflicts, threats, problems, difficulties and unknown allurements. The frontier itself is the place where questions can be asked and experiments carried out.[6] There is also a generally more remote cultural Frontier (which may be distinguished by a capital F) at which entirely new discoveries are being made or sought for, athletic records are being challenged and new art forms are being tried by researchers, athletes, artists and explorers. Teachers will not be knowledgeable about many sectors of this Frontier but they should be acquainted with some, for otherwise they will be unlikely to know what real F problems feel like. The central concepts and rigour of any discipline are maintained by the quality of the work that is done on any particular sector of the Frontier. But the teacher's task is to bring these two creative zones, the learner's and the researcher's, into accord and he does this by posing questions which were once almost unbearably difficult F questions, but which can now be transferred to a context where they are both bearable and inviting to the young—f questions.

As we shall see in subsequent chapters teachers facilitate this transforming work by posing questions and creating opportunities for action. They transform problems from abstract to more concrete modes of representation and this in itself is a kind of creative work which generates meaning. So also any sustained dialogue which occurs between people with different views produces something new. Much of a teacher's work with questions, however, is not a verbal matter at all. As William James taught, every clear concept has a fringe of meanings around it and for children this fringe is often much more interesting—and alarming—than it is for us.

> Every definite image in the mind is steeped and dyed in the free water that flows round it. With it goes the sense of its relations, near and remote, the dying echo of whence it came to us, the dawning sense of whither it is to lead. The significance, the value of the image is all in this halo or penumbra that surrounds and, escorts it.[7]

So all the games we play with children, their skills that we challenge, their doubts and enquiries that we foster, are fringed with questions, with trials and potential errors whose outcome will be punishing or rewarding to them. Our non-verbal behaviour can also be of far-reaching importance for we, like infants, can raise important questions with a movement of the hand or head. The special achievement of psychologists like Bruner and Bower has been to push back the level of scientific enquiry into early childhood by creating ingenious but, at the same time playful, experimental situations which penetrate these fringes and in which children can ask and answer questions long before they have control of the manual or linguistic skills that people normally use to probe their surroundings. Bruner has also given us the outline of a theory which helps us to understand the various levels at which the pedagogic skill of creating the right question situations can be developed. We shall return to this in Chapters 10 and 11.

I once attended a conference of science teachers of middle schools in a rural part of India and we were discussing the difficulty of children questioning, how sometimes questions are asked which threaten the authority of teachers or the status of parents and then one child gets punished and others stop asking. We agreed that, whatever compromises were reached, it was desirable to give questioning itself a built-in place and status in science lessons. One teacher said that he had a system for collecting interesting questions, on some topic like health, and posting up a selection of them each week for discussion. The class would then concentrate on how one could find out the answers rather than on actual answers. Another teacher suggested that at least once a term a BIG QUESTION should be formulated and posted, he meant it to be an F question which as far as the children and teachers could ascertain, was of interest to scientists, but to which nobody in the world has a clear answer.

It is a good but well-worn precept that teachers ought to be able to admit ignorance and strange that this still has to be reiterated. Popular thinking on education is still dominated by the view of the teacher 'who knows' and a big problem of teacher education is to discover ways of getting a young teacher to adopt the more honest and exciting role of being someone who 'knows how' and even more who 'knows how to ask'. This is not a matter of firing questions at the back row, but of genuinely opening up class-room knowledge to all the problem areas and resources of a school, and beyond.

NOTES

1. Autobiographical Essay, quoted in J. R. Bernstein, *Einstein* (Collins, London 1973), p. 69.
2. 'Early learning and behaviour', *Times Literary Supplement*, 7 May 1971. For a fuller discussion of these views see Bower's *Development in Infancy* (Freeman, 1974) and for a wider survey see *Child Slive*, ed., Roger Lewin (Temple Smith, 1975).
3. See, for example, letter by Harry McGurk commenting on Bower's 'Competent Newborns' (*New Scientist*, March 14 and 28, 1974).
4. Premack, Ann and David, *Scientific American*, October 1972, pp. 92–99. The parallel work of R. A. and B. T. Gardner with Washoe is also of great interest. 'Teaching sign language to a chimpanzee', *Science*, N. Y., 165, pp. 664–72. In some ways this is more important because Washoe and Co. make their signs by gestures; Sarah and Co. use signs ready-made. The Gardners found, more recently, that when new human recruits to the project were acquiring sign language, the more experienced chimpanzees slowed down their own speed to help the newcomers, who were a little put out when they realized who was making the allowances.
5. For a discussion of a child's right to ask questions see Elam, S., ed., *Education and the Structure of Knowledge*, especially N. R. Hanson's remarks on 'What is gravity?', pp. 179–80.
6. for some essays on this subject see my *Reconnaissance on an Educational Frontier* (O.U.P., 1970) and also Bourdieu who uses the term *'project createur'* for my 'frontier'. See his 'Intellectual Field and Creative Project in *Knowledge and Control*, ed. M.F.D. Young.
7. *Principles of Psychology*, pp. 254–5. Approaching questions from a different perspective Karl Popper writes in 'The Two Faces of Common Sense', p. 63, *Objective Knowledge* (O.U.P., 1972) 'The central mistake [in the *tabula rasa* or common sense theory of knowledge] is the assumption that we are engaged on *the quest for certainty*.'

CHAPTER 3

Sterile Theory

The world of linguistic empiricists has an extraordinarily glacial, emaciated and sterile character ... Like a diet consisting entirely of disinfectant, it may preserve you from poisoning, but only at the expense of starvation.

E. L. Mascall[1]

The person at the centre of British educational philosophy is *one who knows*, and who appears to be content with that knowledge. Unlike the new-born infant at one end of the scale and Socrates or Gandhi at the other this person is not essentially a questioner and an explorer; he is *an educated man* or, which is even sadder, he is a morally educated man. 'We might say', write Professors Hirst and Peters in the one philosophy book which is required reading in almost every education course in Britain, 'that Gandhi or Gauguin were developed human beings because they displayed some excellence [!]; but they would not necessarily be educated men ..... Conversely we might describe a person as an educated man even if he did not display any human excellence.'[2] This is all very strange. Why make such a concept central when it is so vacuous? It is true that a few lines further down the authors warn us not to take these distinctions too seriously. Nevertheless, the notion of someone who has achieved the state of having become *educated* does pervade Hirst's and Peters' writings and it helps both to keep their own philosophical problems static and to turn the attention of teachers generally away from the nature of the process of education which is of an essentially problematic and inter-personal character. Indeed it tends to focus our thinking on relatively sterile problems about words and status.

In the chapters which follow we can only do a little to open up the implications of putting an enquiring man at the centre of educational thought in place of the knowing one who sits there at the moment. In the present chapter we point to two particular tendencies in the received philosophy of education, both of which make it difficult to see the educational process in sufficiently dynamic terms:

i. There is the tendency to diminish the personal element by reification of human processes, turning these into thing-like concepts and by assuming that children have education *done to them*, that they 'are socialized', rather than they become, or discover themselves in the social world.
ii. We are offered an epistemology which presents an arbitrary map of

knowledge, based more or less on current western conventions and insufficiently open to change.

The first tendency encourages a passive concept of human beings, the second leads to a static view of human knowledge. Such a static view would almost certainly not be defended by these philosophers; nevertheless this is where their kind of philosophizing seems to lead. It is with the hope that more people will see beyond such conclusions that this critical chapter is written. Peters says many wise things but too often interesting and important vistas are blocked by an impressive cliché or a dismissive phrase. He does not deny that heuristic methods have value, but he ignores the theoretical challenge which they pose. Yet despite all this, deeper and more subtle ways of looking at children are already making their way into sociological and psychological thought. Our educatioal philosophy must become more comprehensive if these perspectives, which see men as essentially enquiring, and knowledge as constantly generating new forms, are to be accommodated. Even though such an approach brings in new problems and difficulties it can make the task of teaching more worth while.

A teacher who leaves school for a period of study and who turns to the writings of contemporary philosophers of education for illumination of his problems can find the experience disconcerting. The shallows are entered with a flourish, the deeps are generally ignored. In the world of school there is so much doubt and stress, so much unexpected anxiety and happy confusion, that the assumed clarities and alleged logic of education make us non-philosopher teachers feel guilty about being perplexed. Maybe our philosophers do not actually *deny* the existence of paradoxes and conflicts, but if anybody is going to be caught holding the mysterious parcel when the music stops, it won't be them.

KEEPING THE PERSON OUT

One of the best-worn current educational maxims is Peters' phrase about education being initiation into worthwhile activities. The following passage is from one of his essays on the subject.

'... The procedures of a discipline can only be mastered by an exploration of the established content under the guidance of one who has already been initiated.

In these differentiated modes of thought and awareness both the content and the procedures are intersubjective. A body of knowledge is an accumulated heritage that has stood up to public scrutiny and dicussion and which has structured the outlook of countless men and women with its built-in conceptual scheme. The critical procedures by means of which established content is assessed, revised and adapted to new discoveries, presupposes public principles that stand as impersonal standards to which both teacher and learner must give their allegiance. In science or philosophy it is truth that matters; in morals it is justice as well; in religion it is reverence for the natural order. These fundamental principles mark out "the holy ground" of which D. H. Lawrence spoke.'[3]

Two interesting characteristics of these paragraphs are, firstly the way they are depersonalized, and secondly the manner in which Peters blocks off problem areas as, for example, his reference to intersubjective procedures. Elsewhere he often refers to 'respect for persons' but the central problem of what goes on between people when they argue, teach, trust or enquire, is here politely screened. Yet all these difficulties of mutual learning have been partly explored by phenomenologists and social psychologists. There is only a faint suggestion that theories are provisional, no hint of the disarray which often precedes a scientific advance, scarcely a word about the paradoxes of philosophy or the conflicting claims of truth and justice or of the powerful mystery of religion.[4]

Consider some phrases in detail: 'The procedures are mastered ... under the guidance of one who has already been initiated.' Peters is right to point to initiation as a key concept, but why does he not explore it? Why not at least point out the problems which the word conceals? Why the passive mood? Why must one *be* initiated? Why not 'become initiated'? Or is the distinction between being inside or outside really justified? Are we not all at varying stages of 'becoming' and 'in-ness'? What do the guide and guided ones share? Or not share? And what do they exchange ... 'facts' or ... what? How do they see each other?

Then '... a body of knowledge (thing) is an accumulated heritage (thing) a *built-in* conceptual scheme (mechanical) ... which has structured the outlook of countless men and women.' Would it not be nearer the truth to regard the countless men and women, all of them in varying degrees, as *the people who structure knowledge* and so eliminate these 'things' which are posing as agents? Knowledge would then be seen as a process generated by people, not as a force outside them.

Or what of ' ... The critical procedures ... by which established content is assessed and revised and adapted to new discoveries ...'? This might apply to those rather dull epochs when the leaders of a discipline are not disposed to alter the basic framework of their knowledge. The difficulty here is that the value we place on particular criteria and on different procedures of assessment is itself liable to change. Through his book, *The Structure of Scientific Revolutions*, Thomas Kuhn has been influential in drawing attention to these difficulties.[5] Kuhn shows how a characteristic framework of thought—what he calls a paradigm—becomes established by some major scientific discovery or insight and that this then establishes, for many years, the generalized pattern of how science is done and what kind of questions are asked. The most powerful example of such a 'typical' way of thinking has been the Newtonian paradigm. The new paradigm of relativity does not disprove Newtonian physics, but incorporates it in a wider explanatory framework, which ties up many of the old loose ends, but does not, by so doing, become entirely tidy and unassailable. Karl Popper[6] indeed would say that assailability is essential and he would also stress a more gradualist process than Kuhn. But many philosophers of science would accept that there are such shifting and developing paradigms and that the evolution of scientific knowledge involves great changes in *how* we understand as well as in what we understand.

Then again, why does Peters say that standards must be impersonal? Certainly a sense of truth and a capacity for detachment are important, particularly at times of revolutionary change when emotions run high, but in actual crises, of which one has first-hand knowledge, standards and critical procedures are embodied in people, either in special groups or in one person, who has cherished and exercised them. Such people not only have a capacity for confronting mysteries and playing with problems but they may also possess a rather sceptical attitude towards those very 'procedures by which established content is assessed, revised and adapted to new discoveries.'

In moral questions it is the same story: of course justice and truth are important qualities, but in actual moral crises these are likely to be obscured or even to appear to conflict. The successful resolution of a moral crisis generally involves somebody having an unusually powerful respect for the rights and potentialities of the people involved and perhaps even an apparently irrational constancy to an ideal embodied in a person or in a tradition sustained by people. After the crisis has passed an observer may come along and say, 'Ah yes, I see that justice has triumphed' or, 'Here we have a morally educated man'. But it is precisely from this retrospective viewpoint that many of our educational philosophers concentrate on the wrong questions, analytical questions about the reasons for moral decision. They give the impression that moral principles, moral firmness or flexibility, can be adequately understood as a rational choice. Up to a point, undoubtedly, they can. But the philosophers fail us when they imply that serious discussion should not go beyond that rational point. I shall argue that it is precisely at such frontiers, where clear-cut reasoning falters and where action and imagination, reason and emotion, cannot be kept separate, that education becomes interesting and difficult.

Peters' skill in eliminating the personal and the problematic is also demonstrated by his handling of religion. His reference to Lawrence's 'holy ground' is another subtle piece of blocking. It may be reasonable, in this context, for him not to talk of God and to consider religion at a 'primitive' level, where it is supposed to grow in the field of man-against-nature. But the conclusion of the sentence where he says what it is that matters in religion is startlingly inadequate. What matters is not a feeling of reverence, for religion is, among other things, the response to that. D. Z. Phillips deals firmly with this question of 'the contingency of the natural order' when criticising an almost identical statement by Hirst.

> As far as the feeling of contingency is concerned, the feeling that we could be crushed at any moment, destroyed as persons, by external circum-

stances, that in itself is not a religious feeling. But that response need not be forthcoming, and the feeling of contingency may simply paralyse and terrorize a person. So to speak about a feeling of contingency is not necessarily to speak of religious beliefs at all. [7]

The underlying view is that we conform to moulds and respond to stimuli. The moulds are supposed to be civilized ones and the stimuli may be enobling. But men and women who innovate, who break the moulds in order to make new ones and children who persists in asking awkward questions—these are not given a hearing.

ROUGH GROUND

One of the difficulties about Peters' initial statement at the beginning of this chapter is that it is only a half truth.

The procedures of a discipline can only be mastered by an exploration of the established content under the guidance of one who has already been initiated.

It sounds too much like a closed shop. If we open up these phrases to accommodate wider ideas on authority, skill and discovery which, thanks to writers like Polanyi and Popper, have been gaining currency in the last twenty years, then a more interesting and educationally more challenging statement can be made. I wonder if Peters would object to this:

The procedures and the sense of commitment which characterize those who work in a discipline should be acquired, not only by familiarity with the established content, but also by exploring some of the real problems, which fringe every discipline, under the guidance of one who is already grappling with them.

Peters is trying to conserve and enhance our respect for intellectual values and for proper authority. This certainly needs doing and there *is* a threat from the philistines. The child-centred, heuristic, progressivist vogue has led to excesses; but so, for much longer, has the old fact-ridden, teacher-dominated approach. The educational philosophers do not deny the value of a questioning approach in children; but there is generally a suggestion in their writings that the approach is essentially to what is known and established.

Hirst and Peters do point out, however, that there is no need for us to become locked in a binary conflict over these opposite viewpoints and that there is a synthesis to be attempted, in which both creativity and structure have their place. They are right: but when they attempt to develop this dialectic they fail. The synthesis which they offer arises '... out of the thesis of authoritarianism and the antithesis of child-centred education, [and the synthesis makes] explicit the role of public modes of experience.'[8] What a denouement! It is like telling the Bolsheviks not to walk on the grass. For what are these modes of experience? We are assured elsewhere in *The Logic of Education* that 'detailed studies suggest that some seven areas [of knowledge] can be distinguished, each of which necessarily involves the use of concepts of a particular kind and a distinctive type of test for its objective claims.'[9]

I set out two slightly variant lists showing these forms of knowledge— Hirst's of 1965[10] and the revised Hirst and Peters version of 1970.[11]

Forms of knowledge and experience

Hirst (1965)	Hirst and Peters (1970)
1. Mathematics	1. Mathematics
2. Physical sciences	2. Physical sciences
3. Human sciences	3. 'Knowledge of our own and other people's minds'
4. History	4. Morality
5. Religion	5. Aesthetics
6. Literature and the fine arts	6. Religion
7. Philosophy	7. Philosophy

There are many points that could be raised about these lists; but I think we ought to question the whole enterprise which cuts a cross-section through current 'knowledge' and then classifies it. The authors admit that 'other domains might, in due course, come to be distinguished'[12] but they fail to recognize that such shifts are happening now and should be of great interest to teachers. Further, the overlapping nature of these categories makes them of little use for any theory of knowledge and only of slight value in guiding curriculum planning. Even when discussing these 'forms' on which they try to hang so much, the authors are very cautious when they move away from the relatively firm ground of mathematics and the physical sciences, to aesthetics for instance—'much philosophical work remains to be done here'. Their caution is well justified, for the fundamental point which they ignore is that wherever original work is being done, in mathematics and science, but more so in the arts and in religion, the pioneers show scant regard for customary forms of thought or for 'territorial' integrity. Images and metaphors, models and concepts from many disciplines are exchanged and tried out by those who work on the frontiers, and yet this does not mean that they abandon their commitment to discovering new forms of truth.[13] Because many of our English educational philosophers are so little interested in these frontiers of human endeavour, their knowledge, alas, is mainly of the establishment and their wisdom is conventional.

This situation is made sadder by the ready availability of alternative views which only rarely appear in the fare of teachers under training. Polanyi, Popper and Kuhn are not wild radicals calling for disruption or denying tolerance and authority. Popper has been teaching the western world that it is adventurous and skilful guesswork that provide starting points and that the creation of vulnerable, checkable hypotheses is what leads to scientific advance. Peters often speaks of 'getting inside of' ways of thought but he never explores this interesting phrase. Yet behind it lie fascinating problems, which have been partially unravelled by Polanyi with his exploration of the working of 'tacit knowledge'—that is knowledge that we can use, without necessarily being able to verbalize it.[14] Kuhn's 'scientific revolutions' are readily explorable in terms of Piaget's concept of radical accommodation to new cognitive patterns, and the disputes relating to each can be seen as pointing to deeper issues. (See Chapter 11)

Wittgenstein makes a powerful plea for philosophers to turn towards the rougher ground in his *Philosophical Investigations*. These were written, late in life, after he had spent many of his earlier years exploring the crystalline, logical qualities of language. But he turned eventually to an examination of the other side, to the idea that meaning is a process rather than a state inside our heads. He writes in words which, to me, are both difficult and encouraging:

> 'The more narrowly we examine language, the sharper becomes the conflict between it and our requirements. (For the crystalline purity of logic, was, of course, not a *result of investigation*: it was a requirement.) The conflict becomes intolerable; the requirement is now in danger of becoming empty.—We have got onto slippery ice where there is no friction and so in a certain sense the conditions are ideal, but also, just because of that, we are unable to walk. We want to walk; so we need *friction*. Back to the rough ground.'[15]

I speak as a schoolmaster who came into the world of educational theory in middle age, looking for some comprehensive view. But the books that were being offered to students in the name of educational philosophy seemed generally both limiting and dull—curiously unrelated to my recollection of what actually happened in school. Sometimes students of education—mature graduates and often experienced teachers—are even advised not to venture into rough ground, in case they encounter 'difficult philosophy'. Yet this is precisely what we ought to be doing. The next two chapters are steps in this direction—moves in the process described by Whitehead as stretching our metaphysical ideas. We turn first, and a little gingerly, to the concepts of phenomenology, to the impact of such thinking on psychology and sociology and then, in the central section of the book, we shall look at some other theoretical components which the biological sciences and systems theory have made available.

NOTES

1. *Words and Images* (Longmans Green, London, 1957), p. 75.
2. Hirst, P. H. and Peters, R. S. *The Logic of Education* (Routledge and Kegan Paul, London, 1970), p. 58. But restive voices are to be heard. See David Adelstein in

Counter Course, ed. Pateman, T. (Penguin Books, Harmsworth, 1972), pp. 115–139. He makes some important criticisms of Peters but occasionally becomes vituperative.

3. *Ethics and Education*, p. 54 'Education as Initiation'. Beyond my small criticisms of this viewpoint stands a vast educational question: What is initiation? A question for interdisciplinary attack by linguists, anthropologists, psychologists *and* philosophers. In subsequent writing Peters does not seem to have carried the matter much further. In 'Personal Understanding and Personal Relations' *Psychology and Ethical Development* (Allen and Unwin, 1974) he presents a developmental scheme, based on Kohlberg, but he maintains, nevertheless, a curiously atomistic notion of teaching, benevolence and relationship. See, for example, p. 397.

4. An example of this dismissive blocking is Hirst's and Peters' contemptuous treatment of Martin Buber's important distinction between personal encounters ('I–thou') and thing-like encounters ('I–it') on p. 50 of *The Logic of Education* 'A murky field . . . occupied by the devotees of the various brands of psycho-analysis'.

5. *Op. Cit.* (University of Chicago Press, 1970 (1962)).

6. *The Logic of Scientific Discovery* (Hutchinson, London, 1959). *Objective Knowledge: An Evolutionary Approach* (O.U.P., 1972).

7. Phillips, D. Z., 'Philosophy and Religious Education' in *Faith and Philosophical Enquiry* (Routledge and Kegan Paul, London, 1970), p. 165. This essay criticizes Hirst's 'Morals, Religion and the Maintained School', *British Journal of Educational Studies* 14 (1965–6), p. 7.

8. *The Logic of Education*, p. 42.

9. *Op. Cit.*, p. 63.

10. 'Liberal Education and the Nature of Knowledge' in Archambault, R. D. (Routledge and Kegan Paul, London, 1965) *Philosophical Analysis and Education*, p. 131.

11. *Op. Cit.*, pp. 63–4.

12. *Logic of Education*, p. 65. Hirst expands and defends these views in several papers published in *Knowledge and the Curriculum* (Routledge, Kegan, Paul, 1975). His 'forms of knowledge' are here so well hedged about by qualifications that they appear both less interesting and less obviously vulnerable.

13. An interesting example is Professor Richard Gregory (neurophysiologist and psychologist) and Professor E. M. Gombrich (art historian and philosopher) who have edited a joint work *Illusion in Nature and Art*. The latter has worked closely with Sir Karl Popper and the former has recently contributed an article to *New Society* (May 23, 1974, p. 439) on psychology as 'a science of fiction' in which he explores the idea that the central concern of psychologists should be man's capacity to *invent*— hypotheses, stories, myths.

14. Polanyi, M. *Personal Knowledge*, especially Chapter IV.

15. Wittgenstein, L. *Philosophical Investigations* (Basil Blackwell, Oxford, 1953), p. 34, § 107.

CHAPTER 4

The Perspective of Phenomenology

> Turf was the evolving response of the vegetation to the evolution of the horse. It is the *context* which evolves.
>
> Gregory Bateson[1]

When any teacher passes through one of those periods of professional crisis which come the way of most of us, he may be dimly and painfully aware that he himself is learning. Perhaps he has just started in a new post at a Comprehensive School, which falls rather short of his ideal. At times he feels that the best he can hope for is just to survive this day, or this week. There are occasional respites: with colleagues in a nearby pub, or sudden discoveries of friendships in unexpected situations. Eventually, however, with a good deal of stoicism, the year is survived. A few wrinkles are acquired; some of last year's schemes of work will do for next year and new ideas are simmering: gradually it all becomes more serene for a while.

What is the perspective of a philosophically inclined teacher who endures such an ordeal and reflects on what is happening? He is well aware that he is going to be rather a different person when the storm is over. It will be hard for him to sustain an empiricist's view, observing and recording with consistent objectivity. Conceptual clarity may be of value when he is trying to explain the outcome of his ordeal; but at other times the very issues that need coming to terms with are conflicts deeply felt and with no prospect of rational solution. If, however, he believes in getting involved, in choice and action and in the increased awareness of himself, of be-ing, which such action brings, he might then call himself some kind of existentialist. But this, though an interesting term, is a very wide one which sometimes suggests an anti-rational attitude. There is a related philosophical perspective, that of phenomenology, which shares the person-centred element of existentialism but whose roots spread more widely in the soil of European thought. The very length of the word and the breadth of its connotation are liabilities. In its less abstract forms it is relevant to many educational encounters, for it describes the stance of someone who knows that his own viewpoint is changing, that the context in which he works is changing, yet who still wants to make sense of the processes in which he is involved. It also points to the idea, central to the argument of this book, that meanings are generated by interaction of people with things and with each other. This way of thinking has already made its mark on sociology and social psychology and in the present chapter an approach to some of the less abstract levels of phenomenology will be outlined. Edo Pivčević introduces the term thus:

> Phenomenology is concerned primarily with experiences and their structure; in this it is conspicuously different from modern analytic philosophy which is concerned primarily with the analysis of *propositions*. This however does not mean that phenomenology is not interested in language. Quite the contrary, the preoccupation with language is an important feature of phenomenological investigations. But the emphasis remains on experiences. The structure of linguistic expression...cannot be adequately understood without an analysis of the structure of the experience that makes these expressions meaningful. A sign or a configuration of signs is brought to life in an act of understanding. Without such an act no sign can mean anything.[2]

So phenomenology is not merely, as the word suggests 'discourse about the appearances that come to us'; it refers to the whole process by which we construe this world of appearances; and it is deeply concerned with the meanings which come from our intentional actions and from the things—signs, toys and tools—that we use to bring about joint action.

In this modest sense, phenomenology would seem to offer a helpful perspective for understanding the interaction of teachers and children. But a general warning needs to be sounded, both in regard to phenomenology and in regard to the approach of this book. It would be wrong for the reader to assume that the perspective outlined here represents more than the *influence* of phenomenological thought on the social sciences. In a similar way one takes the influence of Freud's perspective without necessarily accepting, or even understanding, the whole psycho-analytic edifice. Theory can become very abstruse. Sometimes, no doubt, it *has* to be difficult. At other times, the ordinary reader may be forgiven for wondering whether the theorists might not maintain better communication with the ground. When I fail to understand much of the theories of relativity I can readily believe that this is due to my limitations; but when I flounder, up to my neck, in Husserl's brackets within brackets or Merleau-Ponty's difficult rhetoric, I wonder whether it may not be partly their fault. Any teacher, or similar non-specialist, who starts exploring the theoretical disciplines which bear on his work, should be prepared both to use what seem to be the helpful insights of his mentors *and* to treat with some reserve their remoter flights. A corollary of this is that we keep entirely open the question of whether they are rarified or we are dense, or both. We should also remember that philosophical perspectives need not be mutually exclusive. Indeed the analytical philosophers, whom we have just been criticizing, have a useful function when they make us more critical of language that we use and more aware of different categories of thought.

PERSONS IN SOCIETY

One of the foremost exponents of phenomenology in the United States was Alfred Schutz who was a student both of Husserl and Weber. His influence, especially on the social sciences, has been considerable and though he wrote little which referred directly to education, many of his papers are to do with the sociology of knowledge and with the experience of people learning in a group.[3] His ideas, reacting with and developing from some of his better-known predecessors such as William James, John Dewey and George Herbert Mead deserve a more important place in the theory of education. In this chapter I cannot do more than indicate the kind of intersubjective world which Schutz is mapping.

In his paper 'Projects for Action' Schutz discusses what he calls 'the world taken for granted', that is the world which we accept 'as given ... until further notice', until our experience leads us to construe it differently. It is worth noting in advance some of the elements of which Schutz's thought is compounded. For example:

1. Experience is the foundation of action.
2. This is known in a person's biographically determined situation, which yet contains within it areas of freedom.
3. That these are given direction by a person's prevailing interest.
4. The way a person views the world is partly a matter of how he shapes these interests, a matter of construing it or making constructs of perceived phenomena.
5. The project and intentions by which a person is oriented he calls 'in-order-to' motives, in distinction from retrospective and explanatory 'because' motives.

Notice how Schutz's thought hovers on the borders of philosophy, sociology and psychology. In the passage below he is asking 'What constitutes my purpose at this particular moment?'

> This question leads us to the second set of our experiences upon which the practicability of future actions is founded. It consists of the experiences which I, the actor, have of my biographically determined situation at the moment of any projecting. To this biographically determined situation belongs not only my position in space, time, and society, but also my experience that some of the elements of the world taken for granted are imposed upon me, while others, are either within my control or capable of being brought within my control and, thus...modifiable. ... This factor is of great importance for our problem because all my projecting is based upon the assumption that any action occurring within the sector of the world under my actual or potential control will be practicable. But that is not all. At any given moment of my biographically determined situation I am merely concerned with some elements, or some aspects of both sectors of the world taken for granted, that within and that outside my control. My prevailing interest—or more precisely the prevailing system

of my interests, since there is no such thing as an isolated interest—determines the nature of such a selection. This statement holds good independently of the precise meaning given to the term 'interest' and independently also of the assumption made as to the origin of the system of interests.[4]

At this point Schutz inserts a footnote which summarizes a crucial and characteristic distincition:

> Because what is commonly called interest is one of the basic features of human nature, the term will necessarily mean different things to different philosophers in accordance with their basic conception of human existence in the world. We venture to suggest that the various solutions offered for the explanation of the origin of interests might be grouped into two types: one which is concerned with the *because motives*, the other with the *in-order-to motives* constituting the so called interests.[5]

This radical distinction between causal motivation and that kind of in-order-to deliberation which precedes personal acts was not original. The distinction has a long history but tends to be overlooked, partly no doubt because of the ambiguity of the word 'because' which allows it to point forwards or backwards in time. Schutz adopts the backward, causal, connotation. Elsewhere he suggests that only when we explore the first kind of interest, that is, when we trace out one or two causal chains running back into the past and classify what we find there in a system of typical actions—*then* we can claim to be doing social science.[6] When we are facing the other way, towards some future project—and 'we' in the educational sense is at least one teacher and one child—then we are doing something which cannot be adequately explained in the reductive terminology of contemporary science. The connection between a person's vague apprehension of meaning and the symbolism of words, acts and pictures, is central to the argument of this book. The phenomenological approach allows for the intuition of meaning *and* for analytical science, curtailing the latter's predictive claims, but not its capacity to explain what is and what has been.[7]

There is another important suggestion in the Schutz passage which arises from this. He refers to the 'system of interests' which determine the nature of the possibilities which I select. This points to another distinctive corollary in the application of social science—that of interpretation or hermeneutics. If a teacher or a psycho-therapist is attempting to help a seriously disturbed child (or patient) he will use all his skill and insight to get the child to see real problems and real possibilities available for their solution. If he attempts to predict a course of events, or even to give authoritative explanations of the situation, he will be reducing the child's autonomy; but to help the child to envisage its own realistic field of options is to enhance its autonomy. We assume that such options are available in even trying to help. Whether or not such social action is 'science' may be left an open question.

A central argument of this book derives from the above. When we—children or adults—look ahead to what is difficult and complex we do not rely primarily on analytic procedures, we construe the situation as a whole, projecting on to it a frame of perception and hypothesis. The images that we use in such projections are of a symbolic nature; that is, they refer, at least in part, to what is only vaguely apprehended. We then act in accordance with such unclear intimations and may, or may not, turn back afterwards and with increased clarity, explain our act by causal analysis. The ability to switch between analytical and intuitive mental processes is something which teachers acquire in their normal work. But the need for such phenomenological agility might usefully be more widely recognized. Rommetveit describes this as a 'systematic oscillation between estrangement and empathy'.[8] Educational theory must allow for both.

The place of feeling in educational encounters is relevant here and we will return to it later. However, some terms may be given preliminary clarification. Feeling is an awareness of process, within or outside oneself, which cannot be cognitively contained. A feeling of hunger is more extensive than the thought of hunger. Emotions are the meanings we attach to feelings.[9] Empathy is the rational understanding of other people's feelings (I can, for example, understand your anger without, necessarily, feeling it). The need to teach in such a way that children can enter, imaginatively, into the conflicts and tensions of complex human situations is not given the attention it deserves. The perspective that is being emphasized here concerns both sides: the penetration, through symbolic means, of what is not entirely explainable and the rational, objective approach to what is explainable and also the need for wisdom in judging the difference. We shall amplify this when discussing the structures which characterize social and historical studies.

CONSTRUING REALITY

Certainly the phenomenological label is not in itself important, but it does peg out an area—perhaps too extensive an area—in which teachers can face some deep questions. One can see the influence of this new person-centred philosophy at work in the writings of many who would be unlikely to accept the tag. In the field of psychology George Kelly has been one of these, E. H. Gombrich, in the world of aesthetics, is another.[10] In the nineteen-thirties Evans-Pritchard, working, as nearly as possible, from within the Azande and Nuer communities, was laying the foundations for phenomenological anthropology.[11] A common idea which these share and which relates to Schutz's view of 'interests' is this: that the way we see our world depends on the way we construe it. We construct our images and our sense-making patterns, and through them we learn to experience the world. The same idea has also been given support at the level of sense perception and it has been shown that a sense organ, the eye for example, has to *learn* to see the world and that incoming data are processed and sorted by the retina and by the optic nerve, even before they are signalled to the brain.[12] This is a long way from the concept of the sense organs as passive appertures.

In the field of social psychology this leads to the view that everybody in an encounter, even the psychologist, is helping to construct the scene that is being studied. And this in turn produces an interesting debate about the nature of psychological enquiry.[13] It also helps us to understand many educational pressures and curricular constraints.[14]

AN EXAMPLE

Consider, briefly, a scene with which you may be familiar: a young teacher is driven at last to taking a near-delinquent youth to the deputy head because the latest episode in 4P ended in bloodshed. They sit round a table. The youth construes the situation very largely in terms of a-game-and-a-fight; sometimes it is one, sometimes the other; and this is partly because he has no adequate concept of *referee*. So it is generally he who decides when it is a game and when a fight. The young teacher is an idealist. He construes the drama mainly as a social tragedy and he knows enough of urban England and of this youth's home background to support this view. Recently he has begun to see himself as a possible further victim of the tragedy. He has no sympathy for the notion that the situation is a game and only a little confidence in the power of the law to rectify it. The deputy head, a former county rugby player, sees the operation of the rule of law as central to the school but he also has more sympathy for the game-fight view than for the 'victim of a social tragedy' way of seeing things. On the other hand he has a strong sense of loyalty to colleagues and a somewhat less but still powerful sense of loyalty to the children. There is no need to follow this sketch much further but it illustrates two important ways in which a social encounter develops a complex structure from the inter-action of different people operating with different constructs.[15]

The first generalization we can make is that in a conflict like this there is unlikely to be one absolutely right view and one absolutely wrong view. But the alternative, relativist claim, that 'It's all a question of what you think anyway', is even more dubious. There can be, and usually are, extremely important 'shades of rightness'. The black and white pattern of the contour map may be different in different surveys; but the slope is there all the time. Just how a teacher, or for that matter a manager in an industrial or administrative position, balances distant perspectives against the need for greater sensibility, or institutional requirements against therapeutic ones, will depend on his competence in the art of management; and it *is* an art, even when it is exercised by a knowing and delinquent child. We recognize here a kind of negotiation, a triangle of forces, with each participant pulling towards a particular subjective view of truth. Nevertheless one of them, in this case the deputy head, has, and should have, more pull, or authority, than the others. This kind of relativity works against the assumption that there are always heroes and villains on the scene, but it maintains a sense of the possibility of right action and of an intersubjective search for it.

Secondly, the actors in this triangular scene are not merely determining what should be done, they are also determining how the whole fracas should be understood, both by themselves and by other people in the school. They are in short involved in the establishment of meaning. Furthermore they may be accepting, or learning to accept, that their ways of seeing this event will almost certainly be divergent when the meeting is over. The process of debate will continue, for in schools we work much of our time by handling tensions and conflicts not in the hope of finding 'solutions' but of creating understanding. 'Our every day thoughts', observes Schutz, 'are less interested in the antithesis "true–false" than in the sliding transition "likely–unlikely"'.[16] This is a common experience but it reflects another important part of phenomenological perspective—that of seeing meaning as something which is not only shed by the use of words but is *negotiated* in encounters between people. If we knew that the three people who left a meeting, like the one discussed above, did so with their ways of seeing each other totally unmodified, would we not be right to say that the encounter had been meaningless? This points to a sense in which we shall sometimes use 'meaning' in this book, as a kind of action, especially as joint action. In his *Philosophical Investigations* Wittgenstein often returned to this idea, that a word must become alive through action. 'Every sign by itself is dead. *What* gives it life?—in use it *is* alive. Is life breathed into it then? Or is its life its use?'[17]

Use of language by people *is* its life, its meaning; similarly the use of the patterns of society *is* social life and this also generates meaning. To get this deeper, inter-subjective flavour of the notoriously elusive word 'meaning', it is interesting to substitute for it words of Latin origin with similar semantic spread, for example 'moderating' or 'mediating'. Consider the following phrase employing the three alternative words: 'The m . . . . .g (effect) of the encounter only gradually made itself felt in the community'. These words are of course all different, but switching them around does highlight an aspect of meaning which is often forgotten—that it is generated by intersubjective activity, often of a groping and negotiating kind. In brief, then: a pheno-menologist would be interested in the different ways in which individuals construe encounters, in the interaction of these constructs and in the changes of meaning that such interaction brings about.

If our picture of education had remained in the framework of the physical sciences and of nineteenth century biology, then we would have to envisage the children or learners as evolving 'in response to' the environment with the teacher as part of that environment. But the alternative to such determinism is not necessarily a cloudy free for-all. If, as Gregory Bateson points out, in the quotation at the head of this chapter, the context evolves as well as the horse, then we, as teachers may be free to be aware of the changes happening to us and to choose just how much we are involved or how much we will observe, how much we will act or how much reflect. We have that kind of option, but almost everything we do in a school, whether this be active or passive, will contribute to a complex causal network which is part of the whole meaning-generating system.

John Shotter, in his paper 'The Development of Personal Powers', expresses this paradox forcibly in regard to one of the problems of language. He stresses that, though a person using speech may be aiming at some clear objective, this does not mean that he makes each step according to definite rules.

> To suppose there must be strict rules for using words and sentences "would be like supposing that whenever children play with a ball they play a game according to rules". A sentence is something one *uses* to express one's meaning and it is not an expression of a meaning itself; its meaning is a logical construction to be completed both by oneself and one's listener out of the influences exerted by one's utterance.[18]

This idea that meaning is something that we make out of whatever is available for our purpose will be returned to later. The corresponding idea that our making is constrained, but not predetermined, by a field of possibilities accords with common sense but it has been difficult to accommodate it to an essentially predictive science. Where, in any event, *are* the bounds of predictability?

A number of scientific developments have made the conflict between hard headed science and romantic idealism in education a good deal less acute. We have gradually become aware of the use of field theory in physics and there is a thriving branch of biology which deals with the gradations and influences of morphogenetic fields in shaping embryonic growth and tissue regeneration which we shall touch on in Chapter 9. This is all leading away from a simple, linear view of causation towards more subtle concepts.[19] Against such a scientific background come the suggestions of Ayers, Taylor, and Harré that we develop (or reinstate) a richer concept of causal agency, of things with specific and varied powers which operate throughout a field.[20] This way of thinking makes a break with the narrowly mechanistic frame which has too often confined our thinking about social and cultural processes.

NOTES

1. *Steps to an Ecology of Mind* (Paladin Books, St. Albans, 1973), p. 128.
2. *Husserl and Phenomenology*, p. 13. Pivčević provides a concise and critical view of Husserl's ideas.
3. Berger, Peter, L. and Luckman, T. *Social Construction of Reality* (Allen Lane, Harmondsworth 1967) is useful in introducing this approach. Or see the collection *Knowledge and Control—New Directions in the Sociology of Knowledge*, ed. M. F. D. Young (Collier Macmillan, London, 1971). Schutz himself however is often clearer to read than some of his exponents.
4. Schutz, A. 'Projects of Action', *Collected Papers*, Vol. I, pp. 72, 76. (Martinus Nijhoff, the Hague (1964). The paragraphs that follow are also of interest as they deal with doubting and questioning and include a passage by Dewey on 'deliberation'. See also

30

Aaron V. Cicourel, *Cognitive Sociology* (Penguin, Harmondsworth, 1973) for an appreciation of Schutz and of his distinction between interpreting a situation and explaining it.

5. I have not included the whole footnote which goes on to refer to Leibniz and Bergson in a manner which indicates an interesting line of enquiry which some readers may wish to pursue. The italics are mine.

6. *Collected Papers*, Vol. II, 'Social World and Social Action', pp. 11–19 (Martinus Nijhoff, The Hague, 1964).

7. For an analysis of the parallels and differences between phenomenology and structuralism see John Mepham 'The Structuralist Sciences and Philosophy' in David Robey ed. *Structuralism* (O.U.P., 1973), pp. 104–137.

8. Rommetveit, R. 'Language Games, Syntactic Structures and Hermeneutics' in Israel, J. and Tajfel, H. *The Context of Social Science*, Academic Press (London, 1972), p. 224.

9. For these ideas I am indebted to Suzanne Langer, *Mind, An Essay on Human Feeling*, Vol. I (Johns Hopkins Press, Baltimore, 1967) and to Harré's and Secord's *The Explanation of Social Behaviour* (Basil Blackwell, Oxford, 1973).

10. Gombrich, E. H. *Art and Illusion* (Phaedon, London, 1960) 'The Beholder's Share', pp. 181–287.

11. *Witchcraft, Oracles and Magic among the Azande* (O.U.P., 1937) and *The Nuer* (O.U.P., 1940).

12. Gregory, R. L. *Eye and Brain* (Weidenfeld and Nicholson, London, 1966) is an excellent introduction. But for a different analysis, see John M. Kennedy, *The Psychology of Picture Perception* (See notes for Chapter 11).

13. See Harré, R. and Secord, P. F. *Op. Cit.*, pp. 1–64.

14. A lively debate was heralded by the publication in 1971 of M. F. D. Young's compilation *Knowledge and Control*, see Note 3 above. For a contrary view see Richard Pring, 'Knowledge Out of Control' *Education for Teaching*, November 1972.

15. See Richardson, Elizabeth *The Teacher, the School and the Task of Management*(Heinemann, London, 1973), pp. 312–315.

16. *Op. Cit.*

17. *Op. Cit.*,§432.

18. Richards, Martin P. M. ed. *The Integration of a Child into a Social World* (C. U. P., 1974), pp. 238–9.

19. Waddington, C. H. ed. *Towards a Theoretical Biology*, Edinburgh University Press, 1968–9). On a broader canvas see Richards, I. A. *So Much Nearer* (Harcourt Brace, 1968), 'From Criticism to Creation', pp. 3–33.

20. Ayers, M. R. *The Refutation of Determinism* (Methuen, London, 1968). Taylor, R. *Action and Purpose* (Prentice Hall, New York, 1966). Harré, R. *The Principles of Scientific Thinking* (Macmillan, London, 1970).

A version of this Chapter was published in the *Journal of Applied Educational Studies* (Oxford) 1974, Vol. 3, No. 1.

CHAPTER 5

Billiard Balls and After

Alice thought she had never seen such a curious croquet ground in her life: it was all ridges and furrows; the croquet balls were live hedgehogs ...

Lewis Carroll, *Alice in Wonderland.*

Our thinking is profoundly affected by the sediment of words and metaphors that come to us from the past. We cannot escape this but how are we to loosen the hold of such influence? It is a commonplace of the modern wave of phenomcnologically orientated social science that our objectivity should be brought, periodically, under question and that the experimenter himself should be seen as part of the experiment. But this need not mean a slide of science into subjectivity, or of evaluative judgements into an amorphous relativism. For with this current of thought, which accepts the relativity of cultures, run the parallel insights of structuralism, which emphasize the importance of form, not merely at the level of crystals and atoms but at the most complex levels of language and culture. With so many of our intellectual land-marks shifting it is not surprising that we sometimes feel lost; but when we are lost it may not matter provided that we realize the fact and can navigate.

If we reject the simplicities of reductivism on the one hand (after all we're only chemicals aren't we?) and of relativism on the other (after all it's all a matter of custom isn't it?), where can a rational man—teacher, psychologist, theologian or parent—get leverage for his thinking? Three moves are open to us. We might, like the three negotiators in the last chapter, acknowledge that our views *are* all relative and yet recognize, intuitively, that one person is likely to have more experience and authority. Such a move may be sound in the short term but it begs many questions and in the long term it can lead to personality cults and passivity. Then we might say, and this is a move which many contemporary thinkers make, that there are, as yet undiscovered, deep structures, which will contain some scientifically objectifiable truths about the directions and constraints operating on all men and that our task is to elucidate these. Or, thirdly, we might say that there are emergent high-level manifestations of life, like language, in which entirely novel organizations and capacities appear; while we should be interested in tracing the development of such novelties from their biological roots, we must not fall into the reductivist trap of explaining the higher by the lower. This opens up the difficult task of relating values, such as 'better', to degrees of complexity such as 'more highly organized', but we may still think that the effort should be made. In this book I am assuming that both the second and third moves are worth attempting and that they are essentially two aspects of the same process, one being exploratory the other being creative.

In this chapter we shall be discussing the legacy, in social and psychological sciences, of the habit of explaining physical events in terms of hard atoms bouncing against each other like billiard balls. Few leading physicists have regarded this model as having extensive explanatory value since about 1870. But its influence continues to percolate into other layers of thought right up to the present. Closely related to the billiard ball view of physics is the hydraulic model for social and psychological processes. This implies that in all sorts of ways systems are running down and that individual organisms are moving along paths of decay towards equilibrium. Many words and phrases, including some that have gained currency in the popular versions of Freudian thought, display this passive or mechanical connotation. For example 'If he *represses* that *drive* it will only *come out* later in a worse form'. Even when organic metaphors *are* used they are liable to be dead ones. 'One rotten apple will infect the barrel.' Notice how such phrases deny the autonomy of the person. I am not suggesting that we cease to use such terminology entirely, for indeed it may be very appropriate when a person's autonomy *is* diminished—if for instance he is ill or frightened—but we need to be aware of the bias which such decaying and mechanical metaphors create.

But is there anything basically wrong with the billiard ball model and the hydraulic metaphors which 'flow' from it? There is. Billiard balls are made of uniform ivory or plastic in order that their character shall be as uniform and unchanging as possible. If they were live hedgehogs the game would be different; or no game at all. So 'billiard ball thinking' excludes, from the start, the possibility that things have interesting insides or intrinsic powers to influence external events and, perhaps, to change themselves.

Many of the most important scientific discoveries of the last century have been to do with breaking through various versions of billiard ball thinking— radio-activity, atom-splitting, nuclear physics, the discovery of the double helix of DNA and of the genetic 'literature' which it carried.[1] All these have shown how the special characteristics of a thing are related to complex and powerful processes within it. Inside the ball, the molecule or cell there is not 'solid ivory' but something explosive—like nuclear energy or a code. That is why the game sometimes seems to play itself and why, in the long run, even game models are inadequate for understanding animals and people.

The explanation of how the billiard ball model came to dominate western thought is too large a subject to embark on here. It concerns the rapid development in the physical sciences, the effects of technology on popular thinking, the delayed development of biological knowledge and of the influence of a number of interacting philosophical themes.[2]

In recent years however a number of critics of this inadequate paradigm have been making themselves heard. They all share what might be called 'a 'phenomenological doubt' about the possibility of detached observation, doubts which, in the context of physics, were being popularized by Eddington as long ago as 1927.

In the remainder of this Chapter we shall briefly consider the work of two writers who, examining the field from different standpoints, both suggest that we are approaching a 'Copernican' revolution in the human sciences. Though there would be disagreement over just how complete this reorientation is likely to be, there are many writers who see mechanical and physical metaphors and assumptions moving out from central positions in our thought. Words like 'drive', 'stimulus and response' and 'equilibrium seeking' are being questioned, while others like 'system', 'field', 'powers' and 'pathway' are being used to open wider explanatory concepts.[3] The proponents of the new view, whose writings we shall sample, are the late George Kelly, a mathematician who became a psychologist and Rom Harré, a philosopher and historian of science. The common features of their approach which will particularly interest us are: (i) that both have developed a wide theoretical scheme with philosophical and empirical implications; (ii) that they do not accept the conventional view of an objective observer in social science and this leads to a reformulation of ideas on how experimental evidence should be obtained; (iii) both assume a major reorientation of ideas which eliminates the need for any concept of motivation in the social sciences, rather as Galileo and Newton eliminated the concept of 'a mover' or of 'motive force' continuously working on a projectile in order to sustain its flight. Kelly says: 'Suppose we began by assuming that the fundamental thing about life is that it goes on: the going on *is the thing itself*. It isn't that motives *make* a man come alert and do things; his alertness is an aspect of his very being'[4] and it is this which enables him to construe what is coming at him, to *anticipate* events. 'Anticipate' is a favourite word of Kelly's and he uses it in its two popular senses of 'acting in advance' and 'expecting'.

George Kelly died in 1967. His work has been disseminated and interpreted in England by Dr. D. Bannister and now his diagnostic and interpretative techniques are beginning to be used in educational research. One of the important distinctions that Kelly makes is between a concept and a construct. The latter is particularly relevant to our understanding of how people develop different views of the world. The distinction between the concept and construct will be referred to again when we discuss structure in the curriculum. At this stage, however, it is worth quoting Bannister's clarification of the distinction at some length.

A construct is a way in which some things are seen as being alike and yet different from others. A construct is ... essentially a two-ended affair, involving a particular basis for considering likenesses *and* differences *and* at the same time for excluding certain things as irrelevant to the contrast involved. Accordingly, a construct is very different from the logician's notion of a concept. In formal logic, a concept is usually described as a basis for grouping together certain things and distinguishing them from everything else. Thus *black* and *white* would be considered as two concepts and not as aspects of one distinction. *Black* would only be contrasted with *not black*, and *white*, with *not white*. Thus, *dress shoes* might be considered as being just as *not white* as a *good joke* or *a sense of well being*. The idea of relevant contrast and of limited range of applicability or convenience is not involved in the notion of a concept, but is essential to the definition of a construct. The positive statement that a person is *kind* would be meaningless and useless if something were not being negated at the same time. For different people, different contrasts may be involved, (thus one may contrast *kind* with *cruel*, another *kind* with *tough*, or *kind* with *critical*) but for each person the basis of discrimination can only be understood when the nature of the contrast is appreciated. Knowledge of the range of usefulness of the construct is also necessary if it is to be understood adequately. Two people may use the distinction *kind–cruel*, but one may limit its use to describing characteristics of people's behaviour in relation to himself, while the other uses it more broadly to include also natural phenomena like the sea, the weather and his fortunes in life. They may use a similar discrimination, but employ it with very different ranges of convenience.

Sometimes concepts are also regarded as ways in which certain things are *naturally* alike and *really* different from all other things. This use suggests that a concept is being considered as a feature of the nature of things, an inherent categorization of reality. The idea of a construct does not carry with it any such assumption, but rather is seen as an interpretation *imposed upon* events, not carried in the events themselves. The reality of a construct is in its use by a person as a device for making sense of the world and so anticipating it more fully. It must be stressed that all invented dichotomies, however widely agreed (*large–small*), specifically annotated (*bass–treble*), or scientifically approved (*acid–alkali*) are constructs— useful inventions, not facts of nature. The relative predictive value of constructs can be meaningfully explored, but none are absolute truths of nature. . . .

By suggesting that a person can be understood by understanding his construct system Kelly implies, not that a person's constructs are just optional and rather luxurious extras which may sometimes elaborate our understanding of a person's observable behaviours, but that *behaviour* cannot be seen in any meaningful perspective unless the constructions which are being tested by it are appreciated. Kelly sees each man's behaviour as essentially experimental and question-posing, in the man's own terms.[5]

Kelly's basic postulate is this: 'a person's processes are psychologically channellized by the ways in which he anticipates events'. There follow from this eleven corollaries, the first of which is: 'a person anticipates events by construing their replications'. Kelly's language is slanted towards emphasis on the person as agent. His not very euphonious 'channellized' may be intended to be less passive than 'canalized'. The whole system centres on the person as a hypothesis-maker and on the constructs which he makes about the near and more distant future. As Bannister says 'it implies that man is not so much reacting to the past . . . as reaching out for the future: it implies that a man checks how much sense he has made of the world by seeing how well his "sense" enables him to anticipate it: and it implies that a particular man is the kind of sense he makes of the world . . .'[6]

An example of this is that of a wise and fair-minded friend who commented on the last chapter as follows: 'I note again the reference to the deputy head as being more right than the others. I let it pass first time, but feel bound to comment now that it is repeated. . . . Quite a number of your readers are likely to be like me, in having a personal construction of reality which makes them extremely suspicious of deputy heads in general and of deputy head ex-rugby players in particular. I think it might be wise to have a slightly different example.' This raises echoes of the hearty/aesthete dichotomy of the thirties but also of more puzzling tensions. We can be aware of our own constructs and this is particularly important if these have a powerful effect in regard to others. Bannister observes that 'a person who includes himself in the context of the construct, say, *powerful–weak*, binds himself to assess his own behaviour in relation to that dimension. Whether he sees himself as *powerful* or *weak* is of interest to a psychologist, but it is secondary to the fact that the person has ordered himself *with respect* to [that] dimension. From the point of view of personal construct theory, any person, when viewed by another, is regarded as the point of intersection of a number of constructs used by the observer.'[7]

This general approach seems to be in line with our common experience as teachers. Doubtless it is of some help to know that a child's disturbed behaviour is caused by traumas and inadequacies in its past. But in the practical business of dealing with such disturbances we also recognize *that a child fails to see far ahead*, and fails to have the necessary understanding of what he does see. He lacks the social and cognitive skills for coping. No matter how he, or we, construe the past, this oncoming field of the future is where something therapeutic or educational can be done. Sometimes indeed it is necessary for us to re-interpret the past before we can adequately anticipate the future.

The ability of a person to make sense of his world in terms of the contrasting elements of his own pattern, and even to accept its limitations, comes under the general sense of the word 'competence'. This is a key word, as it carries with it the sense of something both inherited from the past and for use now and in the future. It is used in a special sense by linguists as meaning the possession of a certain set of skills necessary for doing something complex or for learning to do it quickly. In Chapter 7 we shall give 'competence' a wider connotation, but for the present we may take it as meaning a thing's powers of behaving or coping in a highly organized way. So we shall now consider a philosophical view which accepts the concept of *powers*—or 'potentiality'—as respectable and important.

INTRINSIC POWERS

What are things, materials and persons really like? Are they like sitting ducks and stationary billiard balls, or are they like loaded guns and sticks of dynamite?

Rom Harré

In his *Principles of Scientific Thinking*[8] Rom Harré outlines a view about causation which goes back, through Kant, to Aristotle. It relates to the intrinsic causal powers which things possess as an aspect of their essential nature. This view makes possible a realistic conceptual framework for the description of natural phenomena and eliminates those artificially mechanistic frameworks into which human sciences are often squeezed. But it requires 'a paradigm shift' a reorientation of the way in which we look at the world. Harré and Secord indicate this when they outline the conventional and the proposed 'modern' bases of science in their recent book, *The Explanation of Social Behaviour*.[9] They contrast the old and the new ways thus:

1. The traditional basis involved two main conceptions, (a) things were considered to be substances with qualities, (b) action was supposed to be impressed on passive things which merely passed it on, the model for this general concept being a passive inert body passing on motion by impact with another like body . . . [i.e. like billiard balls].
2. The modern basis was developed in the late Eighteenth and early Nineteenth Century, under pressure of discoveries of electrical phenomena, and the critical philosophy of physics developed by I. Kant and R. J. Boskovich. It involves a radical revision of thing concepts and action concepts. (a) Things are to be treated as individuals with powers. (b) Action is to be treated as the realization of potentiality created in space in the neighbourhood of active things [i.e. like fields of force].

In the quotation at the head of this page Harré caricatured the two paradigms by which we regard individuals as sitting ducks or billiard balls in the old view or as sticks of dynamite in the new view. He then asked 'why the second paradigm seemed fishy . . . soft occult and mysterious when it seems to be so natural and so clearly forced upon us by the way things are;' why have we got into this billiard ball bias? He then suggests that:

Part of the answer lies in the mistaken epistemology which confines the data, and thus the content, of science to simple truths about sensory qualities manifesting themselves to an observer in particular circumstances . . . It is also partly due to a mistaken metaphysics in which 'power' is seen as a concept surviving from magic, an occult quality appealing only to those of too tender a mind to face the stern truths of empiricism.[10]

Elsewhere Harré and Secord make it clear that this general conceptual scheme 'based upon the concept of power [has] sufficient generality to encompass both electrons and men ... and all degrees of complexity of entity between.'[11] Harré points out that there are also *passive powers or liabilities*— i.e. a thing's 'disposition to suffer change in virtue of its essential nature'.[12] 'In the days when the picture of nature as a crowd of passive sufferers of external and imposed causality was in vogue ... these liabilities ... like "solubility" and "inflammability" ... were the only dispositional properties that ever got mentioned.' Harré also stresses that 'the concepts of power and liability ... are the poles of a spectrum of concepts, distinguished by the relative degree to which we assign responsibility for particular behaviour between intrinsic conditions and external circumstances.'[13] By recognizing the powers of a molecule or an organism, we are not belittling external causal factors, we are setting these in a complementary relationship with internal factors and we are also laying a scientific foundation in which man's power and capacity for action can be understood. It should be noted, however, that Harré does guard against the charge of vitalism, of projecting spiritual substances into material things. He makes it clear that 'to ascribe a power ... is to *open the question of the nature of things, without being obliged to answer it*'.[14] To put it in a simple way this means that we should expect things to have complex internal constitutions which will affect their behaviour under diverse circumstances even if we do not know what these complexities are. We will then be in a position to think about causality in terms of both environmental pushes and pulls *and* in terms of the internal dispositions of a crystal, or a cell or a person. This has a bearing on the way we think about all systems and structures, a topic to which we shall return in Chapters 9 and 10.

In the chapters that follow immediately we shall be moving up and down the scale of complexity as we examine certain aspects of animal and human activity—play, skill, competence for example. As we make such imaginative jumps from a machine, say to a single celled animal or to a human being, it is important to remember that the levels of complexity *are* different and that the words and metaphors which relate them can often generate ambiguities. The foundations for our theory of education involve an attempt to bring together two ways of thinking. On the one hand children do have an incredibly complex 'given' nature whose temporal development, plastic and unreliable though it may be, offers us one dimension for our understanding of education; on the other hand there is a cultural environment which parents and teachers select and shape around those who learn. One is genotypical, with biological roots; the other is phenotypical and has historical and cultural roots. But the interaction is continuous.

An interesting example of this two-sidedness is a person's mental relationship to his own physiological state. Here we have two levels of human activity and from their interaction have arisen a host of philosophical as well as psychological problems.[15] Recent research by S. Schachter[16] lends support to the phenomenological view that we have been taking and illustrates the difficulty of 'levels'. Schachter made careful investigations of people's emotions in relation to their own physiological states. He found that it is sometimes possible for one quite distinct physiological occurrence to be construed in startlingly different ways. He studied, for example, the effects of a sudden increase of adrenalin in the blood on a variety of individuals. A similar increase in one person may cause/accompany panic, and in another it may cause/accompany tension and alertness and in yet another it may cause/accompany a state of religious exaltation. The problem here is indicated by my hesitation about using verbs 'cause' or 'accompany'. Harré and Secord stress that the *interpretation we make* of our felt bodily states has over-riding priority and therefore to use the verb 'cause' would generally be an inadequate description of the situation. Here too it is we who ultimately make sense of our physiological workings. Such interpretation occurs, they say, 'by a restructuring of meaning. When we try to persuade a person to "see" his situation differently, to attend to other aspects of the situation to those he was considering ... If this is true it must be possible for our subject to counter-persuade us to see the matter his way too.'[17] And later they write: 'An emotion is roughly the meaning we give to our felt states of arousal.'[18]

This view of man as essentially a maker, who can make sense of what happens to him internally or who can make a culture from whatever he finds around him, carries some conviction. But it is at variance with much popular science and sociology which sees men largely as victims of their endocrine, environmental or linguistic inheritance. Men are not, in their essence, victims; though that is how we sometimes feel. We have, from the beginning, a kind of freedom, not to do what we like, but to work on the materials—stones, plants, secretions, languages, cultures—which come our way. This freedom is sometimes recognizable as play.

The writers of the Bible and of the Upanishads suggested that God's act of creating the universe was essentially playful, that it was neither done under constraint nor accidentally but as the initiation of some process in which there would be unpredictable and happy splendours. We all know play, not only from our experience as children, but also as adults. We know it, that is, existentially. But as a general phenomenon it is rather mysterious. In the following chapter we will examine some of the manifestations of play in the hope of locating it as a possibly central element of educational theory.

NOTES

1. Neither Watson nor Crick, who achieved the momentous discovery of DNA's structure would be likely to agree with the view that is being put forward here. See J. D. Watson, *The Double Helix* (Weidenfeld and Nicholson, London, 1968).
2. In 1951 Charles E. Raven's Gifford Lectures broke new ground by tracing the strongly

physicalist bias in the post-Copernican period and showing how the lessons of biology were of little influence on the scientific world-view, Vol. I, *Science and Religion* and *Experience and Interpretation* (C.U.P., 1953).

3. See for example Walter Buckley, *Sociology and Modern Systems Thinking* (Prentice Hall, 1967, Englewood Cliffs) or Koestler and Smythies (eds.) *Beyond Reductionism* (Hutchinson, London, 1969), especially Ludwig von Bertalanffy's and C. H. Waddington's contributions.
4. Kelly, G. A. 'Europe's Matrix of Decision' in M. R. Jones, ed. *Nebraska Symposium.*
5. Bannister, D. and Mair, J. M. M. *The Evaluation of Personal Constructs* (Academic Press, London, 1968), pp. 25, 26, 27.
6. For an introduction to Kelly's personal construct theory and an account of its empirical techniques see Bannister, D. and Fransella, Fay, *Inquiring Man* (Penguin Books, Harmondsworth, 1971) on which I have drawn in the above paragraph.
7. Bannister, D. and Mair, J. M. M., *Op. Cit.*, pp. 27–8.
8. *Ibid.*, especially Chapter 10. The above quotation is on p. 268. One may observe, perhaps, that 'clay pigeons' might have served Harré's meaning better than 'sitting ducks'.
9. Harré, R. and Secord, P. F. Introduction to 'The Methodology of the Advanced Sciences' in *The Explanation of Social Behaviour*, Blackwell, Oxford, 1972, pp. 67–68. Though the final phrase is meant to refer to any phenomenon, including atomic particles, it may have a familiar ring to anyone who works in education.
10. *The Principles of Scientific Thinking*, pp. 268, 269.
11. *The Explanation of Social Behaviour.*
12. *The Principles of Scientific Thinking*, p. 272.
13. *Op. Cit.*, p. 273.
14. *The Principles of Scientific Thinking*, p. 283. Parallel arguments in regard to evolution have been put forward by Lancelot Law Whyte in *International Factors in Evolution* (Tavistock, London, 1965).
15. For example see Strawson, P. F. *Individuals* (Methen, London, 1959) Chapter 3.
16. Schachter S. in Advances in *Experimental Social Psychology*, Berkowitz, L. ed. (Academic Press, New York, 1964), pp. 49–80. See also Rachman, S. *The Meaning of Fear* (Penguin Books, Harmondsworth, 1974) where he questions Schachter's methodology.
17. Harré, R. and Secord, P. F. *Explanation of Social Behaviour*, p. 113.
18. *Op. Cit.*, p. 272. But here Harré diverges from Kelly who regards emotion as a misleading and unnecessary concept; see Bannister and Fransella 'Where did emotion go?' in *Enquiring Man*, p. 34.

Part Two

Components of a Theory

CHAPTER 6

Play

Halcyon: Greek derivation: sea + conceiving. 'A bird anciently fabled to breed about the time of the winter solstice in a nest floating on the sea, and to charm the wind and waves so that the sea was then specially calm; usually identified with a species of kingfisher.'

O. E. D.

The word 'play' occurs in a surprising variety of contexts and this may indicate a certain essence underlying all the play-like phenomena of nature. I have a slight hesitation in calling it 'a phenomenon', for play is often best understood as an absence, rather than a presence or an appearance, of something. But whatever it refers to, the word with its manifold uses seems to point to many levels of meaning.[1] My own ideas about play were presented with a clue when watching a film about kingfishers and this opened up some speculation about the simple education which is available to animal young, especially among the higher vertebrates.[2] The kingfisher's behaviour is but one example from ethology, but the name of the bird reverberates with poetic associations— of conception, of calm amidst stress and freedom.

There was one commonplace empirical fact about the young kingfisher's training on which it is interesting to reflect. The fledgling, when it first emerges from its hole in the bank, is endowed with an innate capacity for catching fish with an accuracy of about one in twenty. With training this figure is improved to about seven in twenty. Innate capacity—5 per cent, raised by training to 35 per cent. Here, in the skilled, but not infallible, swoop of the young kingfisher, we have a paradigm for education, the interplay of inherited competence with culturally enhanced skills.

Let us consider this more closely. First of all that 5 per cent is, in human terms, a remarkably high figure for innate success. How often would a young human, even if armed with a spear, have to try before getting a fish? Yet, though in one sense 5 per cent is a high figure, in another sense it is surprisingly low. Bird evolution has been going on for about 500,000,000 years; *then why has not a higher hereditary success rate been achieved*? The skills of insects are sometimes 'programmed' for a much higher level of success and, correspondingly, these insects have less need for laborious learning. Bees and ants are programmed with detailed knowledge of community living and of their particular functions in life. Spiders, at a similar level of evolution, can make a perfect web never having seen one. There are many birds which show a high degree of social transmission of skill. Young oyster catchers take much longer than kingfishers to learn their trade.

There is a paradox here. Can there be too much innate success? Why miss targets? Is it something to do with lengthening and diversifying the learning process? The combination of 'inherent skill 5 per cent 'and 'learnt skill 35 per cent' helps us to see through this problem, which once caused disputes to rage round Jung and now, in different terms has Chomsky at its centre. When Chomsky claims that certain deep elements of language are transmitted by inheritance, he offends against the still widespread billiard ball assumption that children are born almost as *tabula rasa*. Anyone questioning this is liable, even now, to be accused of postulating a process of inherited *ideas*. Jung found himself in a similar difficulty when he developed the concept of archetypes and suggested that certain inherited brain patterns gave a person the possibility of having significant, patterned mental experiences which had not been assimilated as stimuli from the environment.

The truth almost certainly lies in the middle ground. The kingfisher does not inherit the power to live by fishing; it inherits the power to *learn quickly how to fish*. We inherit the power to learn language and this involves the right brain circuitry which the linguists and biophysicists may some day unravel, *and it involves the inheritance of a lot of play and looseness*.[3] Compared with computers we are not only incredibly complex, but also remarkably slack. We inherit specific information through the genetic language of DNA; but we also inherit an open-ness which makes vast subsequent enrichment of the system possible through language and other semiotic or sign systems. The result is an organism which is both open and directional. Both aspects are essential and complementary and for this reason it is futile to get caught up in arguments about nature *versus* nurture.

The analogy which is here suggested between looseness in a machine and playfulness in mammals or humans is, as it stands, superficial. It can be understood at a deeper level if we look at the cybernetic concept of redundancy. For the purposes of this introduction redundancy in a communications system may be taken as meaning 'patterned information, and to spare'. If I wished to communicate an alarm signal to a group of people asleep—children in a boarding house for example—I could tie strings to their toes and virtually pull them out of bed if there was a fire. It could be an almost irresistible, once-only system. Alternatively I might introduce an alarm bell which pinged, not once but in a persistent pattern of pings. This would be a message of higher redundancy. The essence of such a message is that if you only receive part of it there is a good chance of your deducing the rest. The *purpose* of redundancy in a message, however, is:

(a) The message shall not be easily misread.

(b) It shall spread through an appropriate amount of time and space.

(c) It should get a response from recipients who belong to a class and, though they all perceive and decode the signal, it allows for a measure of diversity among them. One may sleep more lightly, another more heavily, one might be in a distant room, another might be slightly deaf.

(d) It allows also for a limited amount of diversity in the organization of the system, and for limited failures to occur.

(e) It allows for higher and lower systems to interact and for the latter to be incorporated into the former.

We should emphasize that any system of communication presupposes some common 'universe of discourse'. The housemaster who sounds the alarm may have wider understanding of the dangers of the situation than the children, but there is sufficient overlap in his and their general experience and knowledge of signal systems for the alarm to work. In short: redundancy in a communication system allows for some measure of diversity and autonomy in the recipients.[4]

This all helps us to understand the nature of youthfulness. The Dutch biologist, Buytendijk, writing in the nineteen thirties, related the concepts of play and of youthfulness in higher animals. Marjorie Grene sums up these views as follows:

> Buytendijk looks at the meaning of the words (chiefly in Dutch and old Dutch) and finds that 'play' connotes a limited freedom of movement, or movement in limited space. More far-reaching in significance for him, however, are visual criteria, and indeed, systematic visual criteria. Actions, he insists, like structures, display a pattern which can be experimentally investigated and scientifically described. It is not directly, however, the pattern of play as such which he now proceeds to describe, but the pattern of *youthfulness*. His first major thesis is that play can be understood only as following necessarily from youthfulness. So it is the systematic visual criteria of the 'youthful' that he is seeking to describe. This does not mean, be it noted, the 'essence of youth': we may find, especially in human beings, occasional 'youthful' characters in an older individual. But where they are, there is play too.[5]

It will now begin to be apparent why, in the higher mammals, play and diversity of behaviour among individuals often goes along with highly patterned, redundant, communication systems. Buytendijk seems to be suggesting that such open-ness is particularly associated with sight and with the images of visual communication. The looser and richer the social and adaptive patterns of individuals in a group, the more elaborate and more redundant must be the communication system which unites them.

POTENTIAL SPACE

Slack in the system, rattling joints and redundancy. It sounds inefficient; yet why is play so serious? The answer can be stated at three levels: in terms of flexibility towards environment; in terms of reciprocity and information flow amongst the species; in more human terms which relate symbol, time and meaning. These we shall now examine.

One might argue that the origins of play could have been to provide a flexible response to the environment, regarding such looseness as an advantage, comparable to the warm blood of mammals, a device for surviving unexpected or unprecedented changes. This does not explain enough and like some other 'adaptive' arguments it is one that easily becomes circular.

Play cannot be adequately understood in terms of an individual and his environment alone. There is no question that men and animals do play alone, but whether they *learn* to play alone is another matter. Sooner or later play involves communication and relatedness. Harlow's studies of infant monkeys mark a turning point in this field. The monkeys were deprived of stimulus from, or interaction with, others and acute symptoms soon developed.[6] So one cannot leave out 'the parents'. It is the group-plus-the-individual plus the context that has evolved. The patterns of environment, of 'culture' and of individual inheritance must overlap and interact and play allows this to happen.

The young kingfisher's initial 5 per cent success is thus the foundation on which further training takes place. With limited ability to survive on its own goes the assumption of *dependence* and this implies youthfulness in kingfishers and a kingfishing culture of sorts which is built onto each individual's basic competence. So teaching and learning become a part of the evolutionary 'edge' possessed by the genus Alcedinidae. It is reasonable to assume that far more information about fishing can be transmitted during this period of dependence than could possibly have been handed over in an 'instant' gene package. So *time* comes in and this must now be considered. We are beginning to see that sometimes 'space' needs to be maintained in a developing system in order that something can happen later. Teleological? Perhaps, but in a very open-ended manner. It will be suggested that one of the functions of highly developed powers of mental imagery is to maintain a similar open-ness in a developing human organism. The following lines were written with a school-boy fisherman in mind, but much of it could apply to the kingfisher which preceded him.

The young hunter holds his desired object in mind night and day and all his actions become animated around the imaginative activity which stretches into the future. This situation, in which the imagined goal is both shadowy and powerful will be familiar ... to those who have taken adventurous but responsible decisions ... The symbolic goal may be more vague, like Columbus's Cathay, or more precise, like Hillary's image of Everest's final ridge, but there will always be a penumbra of uncertainty. And when the goal is reached the image evaporates. In retrospect, it becomes precise, the thing in itself. 'There was nothing to it really' says the hero. But without the imagination and the feelings to generate persistent, haunting symbols, I doubt if a man would take many of the risks his freedom offers ... The symbol does not [necessarily] refer to 'a goal', but to a unique field with many possibilities within it.[7]

The idea that play in all higher animals and art in human societies has a future-orientated function, holding conflict at a tolerable level, and perhaps indicating untried courses is not new but certainly bears on many educational problems. The difficulty is to accommodate such ideas to a contemporary, scientific world-view. This perspective was opened up by thinkers in the continental, neo-Kantian tradition like Ernst Cassirer or Susanne Langer. Cassirer sums up his view of symbols thus:

> Man has ... discovered a new method of adapting himself to his environment. Between the receptor system and the effector system, which are to be found in all animal species, we find a third link which we may describe as the *symbolic system*. This new acquisition transforms the whole of human life. As compared with other animals man lives not merely in a broader reality; he lives so to speak in a new *dimension* of reality. There is an unmistakable difference between organic reactions and human response. In the first case a direct and immediate answer is given to the outward stimulus; in the second case the answer is delayed. It is interpreted and retarded by a slow and complicated process of thought ... Man lives in a symbolic universe. Language, myth, art and religion are part of this universe.[8]

Cassirer was one of the first to regard symbolic activity as being more fundamental even than oral language or tool-making as characterising *homo sapiens*. But he did not, as far as I know, explore the developmental and biological roots of these processes.

Linguists, anthropologists, cyberneticians and child psychologists have been converging for some years on this common ground where play and symbol seem to be related. John Shotter, who is doing research on the symbolic interaction between babies and their mothers, states the case forcibly when he writes: '*the growth of a child of the universe into an autonomous, individual member of a culture takes place essentially in the realm of play*. For the essence of play is that it is an apparently *unnecessary* activity ... (which is) appropriate for later use in the conscious and deliberate pursuit of serious ends.'[9] Elsewhere he explores at length the philosophical implications of shifting play, this 'unnecessary' activity, to the centre of our scheme of thought.

For the last twenty years of his life D. W. Winnicott too was preoccupied with the same focus. He sees the infant's first persistent playing with the corner of a blanket or with a soft toy, 'the first not-me possession', as inaugurating all subsequent cultural activities. He regards these acts of proto-play as being movements away from union and towards separateness. His general term for the first play-things is 'transitional objects' because he sees them as mediating between a narrower and a wider frame of reference. These trivial toys are thus forerunners both of tools and of symbols. Winnicott then asks an awkward, semantic question: *where* is this play activity located? 'I realized', he writes, 'that play is neither a matter of inner psychic reality nor a matter of external reality.'[10] He recognizes that this philosophical difficulty is created partly by the different ways in which adults on the one hand, and infants on the other, construe their joint experience. To cope with the difficulty he coins a new metaphor and says that play takes place in 'potential space' *between* parent and child. The meaning of this phrase can be a little elusive until one realizes that Winnicott is referring to just this sense of 'slack' in a space–time process which we have been discussing. He is referring to a social situation, and he sees space as being created between people to allow for the *possibility of play*— halcyon moments of quiet when causal winds blow gently and we are not driven. I shall be arguing that within such potential space all true education takes place for it is here that potentialities can be realized. Our prime task as teachers is to join with children in the task of creating it and then to understand, enrich and judge it.

With this in mind, we may speculate on the animal origin of these things and recall Lorenz's sticklebacks or Tinbergen's seagulls, each defending its own territory against neighbours.[11] As a seagull moves out from its own territory into that of another bird, its aggressiveness decreases. When two gulls encounter each other on their mutual boundary with equal aggressiveness, deadlock threatens; but it can be avoided. The gull indulges in 'displacement activity'. It strops its beak on the ground, makes nest building gestures of a standardized but curiously inappropriate nature. A reductivist might explain the activity as 'a sink' into which surplus aggressive energy is drained. (These well-loved hydraulic and sanitary metaphors!) But this is surely inadequate. However such displacement activity arose in the first place, we must recognize that it now begins to have 'a meaning'. It is patterned activity with some reference to the future. It makes sense between that pair of birds in terms of their not proceeding to kill each other; it has meaning for the colony as a whole by keeping sufficient space, but not too much, between individuals; and, more remotely, it makes sense in terms of the whole species and its ecological context thriving and surviving. I am not suggesting that birds have awareness of such meaning; rather that we can see here the roots of symbolic action between individuals and 'the sense' that follows it.

We have been considering the concept of play in such a wide range of contexts that there is some danger of forgetting the essence of the word as we contemplate its ubiquity. If we think of play as having a core meaning closely related to looseness and a series of more and more elaborate meanings as this looseness becomes an element in higher and higher levels of systematic organisation, we can think of it becoming a verb of intentional action at the level of consciousness. The levels of 'play's' connotation can now be sketched as follows:

Slack   The word for play in a machine.

Redundancy The word for spare information in a machine or in a brain conceived as a machine. It implies an adaptive capacity or resilience in a complex system which enables it to coexist with others without interference; to be damaged, perhaps, but not easily destroyed.

Open-ness   The word for play in a living system or society.

Playfulness   The word for play in a young animal, particularly as it encounters its environment, but this runs into the next ...

Inter-play   The word for play between animals in a social system, usually expressed by symbolic action (ritual, language, games and liturgy).

Freedom   The word for play when perceived existentially as *scope for making* sense or love or music or even trouble.

I am omitting any consideration of the extensive field of games, rules, routines and rituals, whose bearing on education needs much detailed study. In subsequent chapters some of the problems of symbolic interaction will be returned to. It is worth noting, however, that from the level of stickleback behaviour up to the level of human drama and liturgy, interplay of the members of the species is largely through symbolic action. Such play often involves the following:

(i) It may terminate, or initiate, a phase of action and in so doing it often assumes a ritual form.

(ii) It is often related to boundaries and, via behaviour on boundaries, to rules. But to understand boundaries we need also to think about the organized systems which they delineate.[12]

(iii) It creates a moment of 'space'—time-space—between individuals when territorial space has been used up. This is a point to which we return in Chapter 7 where we will look in greater detail at the idea that competence is a high level power with play (open-ness) incorporated.

(iv) Play in its symbolic aspect handles and makes available information which may be important but which cannot be expressed in clear-cut, instrumental terms.

NOTES

1. Huizinga, J. *Homo Indens* (Routledge and Kegan Paul, London, 1949). Rahner, H. *Man at Play* (Burns Oats, London, 1965).
2. B. B. C. film *The Kingfisher* in the *Private Lives* series.
3. Karl Popper calles it 'plasticity'. He writes: '*I suggest* in addition that *the plasticity* needed for these modifications is also inborn'. *Objective Knowledge* (O.U.P., 1972), p. 71 (his italics). Here Popper uses 'knowledge' in an evolutionary sense very similar to 'competence' as used here.
4. Gregory Bateson goes into this more fully in his 'Cybernetic Explanation' in *Steps to an Ecology of Mind* (Granada Publishing, St. Albans, 1973). His 'A Theory of Play and Fantasy' in the same collection is also of interest.

5. Grene, Marjorie, *Approaches to a Philosophical Biology* (Basic Books, New York, 1965). Her whole essay on Buytendijk is interesting. The four characteristics of youthfulness are given as: (i) want of direction; (ii) the drive to movement, (iii) a *pathic* quality—involvement with *how* one acts rather than with directionality and (iv) shyness. The original is F. J. J. Buytendijk's *Das Spiel bei Mensch und Tier* (1953).

6. 'Development of Affectionate Patterns in Infant Monkeys' in B. M. Foss, ed., *Determinants of Infant Behaviour* (Methuen, London, 1961).

7. Hodgkin, R. A., *Reconnaissance on an Educational Frontier* (O.U.P., 1970). p. 82.

8. Cassirer, E., *An Essay on Man* (Yale University Press, 1944), pp. 24–5. Cassirer uses 'symbol' as it will be used in this book, not as synonymous with 'sign' but as mediating, or bringing to birth, what is new and perhaps 'difficult'.

9. Shotter, John '*Prolegomena to the Study of Play, Journal for the Explanation of Human Behaviour*, Vol. 3, No. 1, April 1973, p. 47. The whole article is of importance to the theme of this book. Shotter outlines in greater detail the philosophical background which has made it difficult to formulate a theory of play and he suggests an alternative framework which is very relevant to education.

10. Winnicott, D. W. *Playing and Reality* (Tavistock Publications London, 1971), Chapter VII.

11. Lorenz, K. *On Aggression*. Tinbergen, N. *Social Behaviour in Animals* (Methuen, London, 1953). While we are making use of ideas borrowed from ethology a warning should be sounded. John Mepham reminds us that 'Human social relations of production and property cannot be understood by an appeal to the phenomena of territoriality among birds. . . . The problem is not to show that culture is part of nature but to show in exactly what ways culture includes but transcends nature.' John Mepham 'The Structuralist Sciences and Philosophy' in *Structuralism*, ed. David Robey (O.U.P., 1973).

12. For a fuller discussion of rule-following and the distinction between this and *regulated* action see Shotter in Richards, M. P. M., ed. *The Integration of a Child into a Social World* (C.U.P., 1974), pp. 68–77. See also pp. 119–20 below.

CHAPTER 7

Competence

... Psychology conceived as 'behavioural science' has been concerned with the behaviour and acquisition or control of behaviour. It has no concept corresponding to 'competence' in the sense in which competence is characterized by generative grammar. ... One important future contribution of the study of language to general psychology may be to focus attention on this gap.

Noam Chomsky[1]

The concept of competence carries a double meaning—of capacities given both for use and for development. We use it both for inherited powers or capacities and in reference to a flexible system which is open to subsequent learning and adaptation. An analogy from the world of business may keep the various distinctions clear: a man inherits a business—machines, buildings, stores. He may then decide to enhance its productivity (competence) or just to let it run (performance); in business as in raising children the art is to strike a good balance between the two. The inherited 'talent' of Christian teaching, that gift which we must use and develop, carries this same two-fold meaning, but it is not one whose implications have often been discussed by psychologists. However in an essay called 'On Voluntary Action', Jerome Bruner[2] develops the idea of competence in a generative system in precisely the way we have been considering. Because the whole matter of skill acquisition is so central to education, his remarks are important.

First of all Bruner distinguishes between ex-afferent and re-afferent operations of a nervous system. If I hold the branch of a tree which is shaking in the wind, various receptors in my skin and joints send out ex-afferent signals to my spinal cord and brain; but if I positively shake the tree, the motions and pressures of my hand will be very similar, but re-afferent signals will come back from my arm to the Central Nervous System which can distinguish one kind of signal from the other. The ex-afferent signals are *information from outside* the C. N. S.; the re-afferent signals are progress reports on the system's response. Bruner then goes on to show that 'there are some systems of action in which the re-afference system, its capacity for control by corollary discharge to related systems, and therefore its "skill" is virtually zero at the outset [e.g. at birth]. The visually guided use of the hands in human beings is ... like this and it is particularly interesting to examine its growth because it reaches such delicate virtuosity after so awkward a start.' Bruner contrasts this with the movements of the eye which, from the start, are smooth and controlled. Then he continues:

> We know extraordinarily little about systems that acquire their organization in contrast to those that have much of it *built in* from the start. I believe that it is of great importance to examine the former type of system with especial care, for it is in such systems that one finds maximum plasticity, a maximum modelling of the most variable features of the environment, and a maximum amount of information processing. These are the systems of action that, I believe, become *generative* in the linguistic sense—capable of being employed in a variety of contexts by the use of a minimum set of elementary operations combined and recombined by rule-governed programmes. I believe it is the open quality of these systems that allows for their incorporation of prosthetic devices and tools on the one hand and of language as a medium for programming action on the other.[3]

Here we have a summary of what competence is—a system in which much is 'given' and much is relatively 'open'. Nevertheless it does appear that this element of 'plasticity' which Bruner introduces, and which I find so important, raises fundamental difficulties which can only be partly resolved in this book. The double formulation is worth pursuing for it allows us to accept both the possibility of inherited basic programmes (deep structure etc.) *and*, particularly with higher vertebrates, of long periods for that cultural enhancement of competence which is sometimes called education. It helps us to understand too why the human infant seems to be born prematurely, 'in order' that the period of interplay, of symbolic interaction, between mother and child may be maximized.

In the first year of life the human infant has to learn to be human, to stand upright, to speak and to acquire the rudiments of rational behaviour. Professor Marjorie Grene, in her discussion of Adolf Portmann's ideas refers to this 'rootedness of man's social life in his *biological* nature ... This integration of man as uniquely cultural animal into a solid biological foundation that enables us ... to see ourselves ... both as human beings and as at home in the natural world: because we are *biologically* formed to be *cultural* animals'.[4] Later she writes:

> The whole structure of the embryo, the whole rhythm of growth, is directed, from first to last, to the emergence of a culture-dwelling animal—an animal not bound within a predetermined ecological niche like the tern or the stag or the dragonfly or even the chimpanzee, but, in its very tissues and organs and aptitudes, born to be *open to its world*, to be able to accept responsibility, to make its own the traditions of a historical past and to remake them into an unforseeable future.[5]

Some readers will remark an incompatible teleological implication in the above paragraphs. Elsewhere Marjorie Grene makes clear that she is not speaking of a goal-seeking evolution but, rather, of a development which is shaped by formal elements—patterns or rules—which guide a process. I would suggest, further, that teleology of an anthropocentric or anti-evolutionary kind can also be avoided if the status of play or, to use her own words, 'openness to the future' is seen as being an important element in the competence of all evolving, high-level organisms.

In discussing the implications of competence we will leave on one side the much-argued matter of linguistic competence, and will illustrate the discussion mainly with skills and artefacts which are much less complex than language. The practical skills which we ourselves have achieved as adolescents or adults are of particular interest for they are to some extent accessible to memory and to introspective observation. We cannot remember the long, though rapid, process of learning our native language, but perhaps we *can* recall how we learnt to climb, to drive a car, or to use a potter's wheel.

Competence cannot be discussed in isolation and the word requires a referent in terms of future activity. Competence may be *for* speech, for driving or perhaps, in a very wide sense, competence for living in the nineteen-eighties. Even in the last example, one would suppose that some specific aptitudes were implied, such as a capacity to deal with complex messages or tolerance of crowds. Unless certain kinds of future action or purposive non-action are implied, the word has no meaning.

It must be stressed too that competence is being used in a wider sense than that of *a power*.[6] Dynamite has the power to explode; so has a temperamental teacher. But as we have seen the kingfisher, the child, the human hand, all came into the world incompletely furnished with programmes of action and the programmes which they did inherit were open enough to permit extensive and adaptive learning. The teacher who loses his temper certainly displays his powers but not his competence. One could say, in such a case, that he had been over-equipped with programmes and under-equipped with 'play'.

To define the concept of competence in this way does not solve many problems, but it has the advantage of shunting them to appropriate levels. For instance: what *are* these innate elements of a skill—the new-born child's prehensile grip, for example? Once the psychologists have established that this phenomenon does occur in new born children it becomes a question for comparative anatomy, for zoology, for physiology and perhaps even for biochemistry. Or: what is the nature of this play or open-ness which competence includes? Are we postulating inborn 'freedom' or what? Such metaphysically formulated questions again point to different levels of discourse. I may feel free when exercising my competence as a mountain climber; but a geneticist might isolate factors in my inheritance which may limit my performance, a psychologist could formulate questions about the interpersonal pressures in my childhood which set me on this hazardous path and a sociologist might describe the constraints of class and culture, or the opportunities of affluence and leisure, which made other openings less likely.

SKILL, TRAINING AND EDUCATION

The word 'skill' will generally be used for narrower fields of action than competence. There are elements of open-ness in both and there is overlap in their reference. Here, however, 'competence' will be used to imply programmes of action and flexibility, oriented towards a wide and varied field; skill will be used when the field is narrower and when specific attainments can be indicated. In education it is often possible to make accurate assessments of whether a person has or has not gained a specific skill; whereas to measure a person's competence—'as a language user' for example—is notoriously hard, even though we are well aware that there are big quantitative differences between high and low levels of achievement. Compare for example the difficulties of examining 'O' level English language with testing typing and stenographic skills.

One other set of frequently argued semantic problems can be clarified here. If it is the task of education to enhance a student's general competence, then we can use the term to distinguish between the wide functions of an educator and the progressively narrower functions of training, indoctrination and brainwashing. According to our usage then—

> *An educator* will be concerned both with extending the positive powers of a person *and* with maintaining his open-ness or existential freedom.
>
> Both *instructor* and *trainer* will be concerned largely with developing a pupil's positive powers, with particular skills or sensitivities, while open-ness and play will be largely ignored. Presumably a trainer is more concerned with practice and rewards while an instructor is concerned to understand and assist the assimilation of the structure of a skill or of a narrow range of concepts.
>
> *An indoctrinator* will not hesitate to reduce a pupil's freedom or open-ness, though he will still try to enhance selected skills and positive powers.
>
> *A brainwasher* will be willing, not only to encroach on his victim's open-ness, but will be prepared to break down his existing powers as well—his power of discriminating between real and imaginary experience for example. An indoctrinator will cramp autonomous development: a brainwasher will try to destroy what has already been built up.

COMPETENCE = 'MOTIVATION'?

In the past fifteen years there has been a perceptible tendency for people to become restive about the word 'motivation' and to recognise its dependence on behaviourist psychology. In 1959 at the Nebraska Symposium on this subject Robert White gave a paper which was in the nature of a turning point and which was entitled 'Motivation Reconsidered: the Concept of Competence'[7] Here he argued that motivation was often used as another word for the operation of competence and that specific internal drives or intrinsic or extrinsic things called motives do not have to be postulated to explain purposive activity.

Behaviourist theory developed largely from strictly controlled laboratory experiments on animals, and this produced much important information about nervous systems. But the resulting psychological theories, especially in the form in which they percolated into popular thinking, did not make nearly enough allowance for the difference between an experimental and a real-life situation. If you allow a rat to become hungry and put it in a maze you will get 'strongly motivated behaviour'. If a rat is hungry in its natural surroundings it will certainly search for food, but it will do other things as well. It will explore, look round for predators, communicate with other rats, clean its face and rest. Searching for food is only part of a wider spectrum of activity and the maze experiment abstracts this from the more extensive, natural pattern.

Robert White sums up his concept of competence in words which echo the halcyon calm of play. He points to the 'biological appropriateness of an arrangement which uses periods of less intense pressure for the development of competence', but he does not entirely exclude conventional motivation, for he continues:

> This is not to say that the narrower but efficient learnings that go with the reduction of strong drives make no contribution to general effectiveness ... but a much greater effectiveness results from having this capacity fed also from learning that takes place in quieter times. It is then that the infant can attend to matters of lesser urgency, exploring the properties of things he does not fear and does not need to eat, learning to gauge the force of his string-pulling when the only penalty for failure is silence on the part of the attached rattle, and generally accumulating for himself a broad knowledge and a broad skill in dealing with his surroundings. ... Perhaps the example of the well-fed baby diligently exploring the several features of his mother's face will serve as a reminder that here, too, there are less urgent moments when learning for its own sake can be given full rein.[8]

More conventional psychologists rely heavily on those specific internal drives which either appear to work autonomously or towards particular external goals. They assume that when an animal lacks some important item, some 'need', there are receptors in its body which signal this deficiency and the animal will set about putting this right. The aim is to establish equilibrium or homeostasis. There is undoubtedly some truth in all this; but it is far from being the whole truth and even non-living systems must be understood in terms which are more active and unpredictable than equilibrium maintenance. So with living creatures, sometimes they are in a state of homeostasis (rest and sleep for example) and at other times they are active, adaptive and innovative. We shall return to this in Chapter 9.

If we are to assume a general exploratory activity[9] in healthy living systems and especially in the higher vertebrates, then interesting questions turn on how such activity may be externally frustrated or how it may be internally channelled. The possession and development of competence for a skill is just such a directional channelling and it does not depend on specific goals and motives, though these are not excluded.

When Mallory made his notorious remark about Everest being 'there' he was fobbing off his questioners with a half truth. It would have been more adequate, though perhaps less modest, had he said that he, and a few others, possessed—just possessed, after long experience—the climbing competence needed to do it and also the imagination to see the summit of Everest on their own individual frontier of achievement. To possess is, on the frontier, to be possessed by.

NOTES

1. *Language and Mind* (Harcourt Brane, New York, 1968), pp. 63–4. Chomsky's definition of competence as what we know implicitly (i.e. generally without knowing that we do) and the contrasting concept of *performance*, is in line with the ideas on structure which I sketch below (Chapters 9 and 10). But my inclusion of 'play' as an element of competence does not rest on any linguistic authority, though Chomsky does leave room for such a possibility: 'the real problem', he says, 'is that of discovering an assumption about innate structure that is sufficiently rich . . .' (*Ibid.*, p. 69).
2. 'On Voluntary Action' in Koestler, A. and Smythies, J. R. (eds.) *Beyond Reductionism* (Hutchinson, London, 1969), p. 162.
3. *Ibid.*, p. 163. The investigation that Bruner then describes and much of his subsequent research has been concerned with the complex oral skills that an infant can acquire by developing sucking techniques.
4. 'The Characters of Living Things', 'The Biological Philosophy of Adolf Portmann' in '*The Understanding of Nature*', pp. 254–293. Boston Studies in the Philosophy of Science XXIII, Synthese Library, Vol. 666 (D. Reidel, Boston, 1974). Marjorie Grene in 'Aristotle and Modern Biology' (*Op. Cit.*) deals with the problem of *telos* and *eidos* in a way which has a relevance also to Chapter 10 below and to the relationship of objectives and formal structure in curriculum, or other, planning.
5. *Ibid.*, p. 228.
6. Shotter, J. 'Natural and Acquired Powers', *Journal for the Explanation of Human Behaviour*.
7. White, R. W. *Psychological Review*, 66, No. 5 (1959).
8. *Ibid.*, p. 327.
9. Sir Percy Nunn, in his *Education its data and First Principles* (Edward Arnold, London, 1920), used the term hormé for this universal exploratory element in living organisms, p. 28.

CHAPTER 8

Toys, Tools and Symbols

> While we rely on a tool or a probe, these are not handled as external objects ... We pour ourselves into them and assimilate them as part of ourselves, the operating persons. We accept them existentially by dwelling in them.
>
> Michael Polanyi[1]

A theory of education should relate mainly to the nurture of human young within a human culture. But there is no reason why its roots should not penetrate the study of all teacher–learner systems and draw on ethology, zoology, physiology and cybernetics. In this chapter I shall sketch the beginnings of such a theory and then develop some of its implications. We may start with the concept, just elaborated, of the inherited competence of a new-born organism, kingfisher or infant on the one hand, and on the other, the culturally transmitted patterns of knowledge and skill which sustain a young organism, and within which it will develop.[2]

The ground which needs to be covered by a theory of education can be set out diagrammatically as follows and it will have to describe, among other things, what happens in the gap.

What goes across the interface? Put briefly: *structure goes one way; search and questioning go the other*. In the diagram these two movements are suggested by the arrow and the question mark. But this leaves out much that goes on

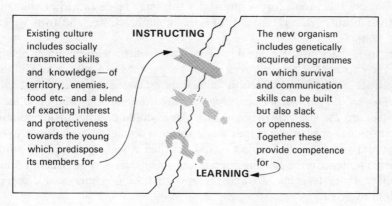

Existing culture includes socially transmitted skills and knowledge — of territory, enemies, food etc. and a blend of exacting interest and protectiveness towards the young which predispose its members for

INSTRUCTING

The new organism includes genetically acquired programmes on which survival and communication skills can be built but also slack or openness. Together these provide competence for

LEARNING

Figure 2. The gap

around learning—all the feelings and intuitions, the hierarchies and necessary delays, the fantasies, frustrations and hard work. As no representation of education would be adequate without at least an indication of these, they are suggested in this preliminary diagram by a severed question mark and a half-formed arrow. Some of the extensive implications of words like 'structure' and 'question' are examined elsewhere (Chapters 2 and 10), but we will now turn our attention to those *things* which, especially in human societies, make possible and amplify this traffic of information—the toys and tools, the symbols and the whole sign system of teaching and learning.

Some animals, apart from humans, possess a culture which includes simple tools. But the probes with which chimpanzees search for ants or the sticks with which they attack a leopard are primitive and are only the rudimentary fore-runners of a flood of artefacts which appears with the emergence of *homo sapiens*.

The educational theory which will now be reconnoitred begins with skills and then turns to objects and their use. It is built round the basic dyad of an older person or animal, the instructor and a younger one, whom we will call the learner. But in this book we barely touch on the wider social field in which education actually takes place and we are avoiding linguistic issues, not merely to keep away from deep water, but also because if a theory of education holds for pre-linguistic human communication it may be subsequently developed as a model for more sophisticated theories. We shall nevertheless bear in mind that language is a super-skill containing many conceptual sub-skills, that words are carefully shaped packets of sound which we throw at each other through the air or which we translate into black and white artefacts on paper. So what we can say about the learning and teaching of simple skills may at least partly be true about super-skills and the artefacts which embody them.

Artefacts are not just *made*. They are first of all things which happen to be lying around—what Levi-strauss calls bricolage—which come to be identified, accidentally or otherwise, and are then made to serve a purpose. They may be shaped and modified so that the purpose is attained more satisfactorily, and then we call them tools (or weapons). Or they may be decorated or cherished for their beauty, emotive power, interest or ambivalence, and then we call them symbols.

Let us go back to the beginning of human artefacts with an infant playing with the corner of a towel. Winnicott, in his paper 'The Location of Cultural Experience', claims that '*When we witness an infant's employment of a transitional object, the first not-me possession, we are witnessing the child's first use of a symbol and the first experience of play*. An essential part of any formulation of transitional phenomena is that we agree never to make the challenge to the baby: 'did you create this object or did you find it lying around?'³ The first, italicized sentence is the starting point of our theory; the second is an important corollary about teaching, art and therapy—that construction and discovery lie close together.

When I first read those phrases in *Playing and Reality* I found the concept of potential space rather confusing. This was partly because it took some time to realize that 'space' meant security and lack of pressure for learner and teacher in *both a spatial and a temporal sense*. Winnicott also, I think, intended 'potential' to refer to the potentialities of the learner which were being realized. Also because this was essentially an interdisciplinary notion, belonging to psychology, sociology, pediatrics and ethology, it was difficult to locate it intellectually. However, I think the concept is important for any unifying theory of education, for it holds together an exploring, but vulnerable learner and, in the same concept, an experienced and protective instructor who is, nevertheless, just as much involved in the process of making space and making sense as is the child.

THEORETICAL OUTLINE

1. *Potential Space and the Emergence of Order.* All learning must take place in *potential space*, that is in an unpressurized place and time. Only in such 'space' can a generative system operate and this is what education is trying to bring about. These ideas could be qualified, in terms of information and systems theory, by saying that learning takes place when there is redundancy, and further that learning is *neg*-entropic (i.e. working away from random chaos) in that it brings about an increase in the orderliness of an individual organism, or between several, by relating them in a larger organization.

2. *The Learner as Doer.* In describing social situations we often make the mistake of emphasizing too much the moulding effect of some Durkheimian space or role into which a learner moves. If we are to avoid the dangers of reifying society and of overworking instrumental and mechanical concepts like *socialization* and *motivation* we must remember Kelly's dictum, 'the fundamental thing about life is that it goes on. It isn't that something *makes* you go.'[4] Potential space should therefore be regarded as a joint creation of mother and child, of teacher and taught; each partner is co-operating, using the other *and* letting it be. In their joint action they press back, but never eliminate, the influence of that more mechanical Dukheimian space which inevitably constrains all of us who live in a social world. Their patterns are overlapping and interlocking but at different levels of complexity. So it is—at levels of much greater disparity—with an artist and his material. Both are patterned: the sculptor much more than his stone, but to some extent he co-operates with it.

3. *Transitional Objects.* We extend Winnicott's general term to cover all cultural artefacts used in the field of potential space—in open situations, which have an element of discovery in them or in which novel constructions are being made. Tools, in so far as they become integrated within a skill to be used in routine procedures, move out of this category. Both tools and symbols have their origin as play-things. But symbols retain their ambivalence, the 'me-not-me' quality of toys and they have some-

thing else, the power of sustaining feeling; but we shall return to this later.

4. *Toys.* Toys are undifferentiated cultural objects which remain in the field of play. They are ambivalent, in the sense just mentioned and also because they may become tools or they may become symbols. But generally among all three there is transition and overlap. A child may just fiddle playfully with a pen-knife at one moment, he may use it, instrumentally, to cut an apple the next and may then weave symbolic fantasies around it. It is use and context which show to which class an artefact belongs.

5. *Play and Skill.* As play becomes purposive it becomes simplified, stronger and more efficient. Successful strategies may become conceptualized as rules and at the same time goals generally become more distant in time and space. Speaking metaphorically one could say that potential space becomes elongated and directional—more a pathway than a play-ground (see Chapter 9). These changes represent the refinement of a learner's patterns of action and with such enhancement we must suppose that there are built up correspondingly efficient patterns of internal circuitry and increased tissue strength in the organism. As a skill becomes more efficient, the element of slack will be largely eliminated from the actual performance. Though even here slack will be cultivated in periods of alert attention or of controlled rest. Observe, for example, the slight playful movements of a tennis professional as he prepares for a 'serious' attack, or the sign of the cross, or the *b'ism illahi* of the Faithful as they embark on some enterprise.

6. *Tools.* Toys become tools as play becomes skill. As most human skills involve elaborate prosthetic extensions to the body, so there must be corresponding internal elaboration of brain circuitry to reflect these complex processes of external tool use. But there is a limit in complexity of the objects we are capable of using externally and so to the skills by which we internalize our control of them. Many of the achievements of technology are in the direction of pushing this limit upwards; and the limit is an important psychological reality none the less. A doll may be a 'mere' toy or it may be used and misused in many ways, but the person whom the doll symbolizes is another matter. When a child tends and cherishes a doll, such play almost certainly has symbolic meaning and this foreshadows roles which may be not realized for twenty years. Such activities are not 'mere' play, nor are they instrumental. I am, at this stage, deliberately passing over a difficulty about how toys change into symbols or tools and we shall return to this in Chapter 11.

7. *Symbols.* Many of the 'objects' in a child's potential space are played with as toys but are too complex or too autonomous ever to be assimilated as tools. Pets often occupy an intermediate position; sometimes they fill an instrumental function and sometimes they are respected 'for themselves'. When a pet or a sibling or parent resists an infant's attempts to use it instrumentally we are not merely witnessing one organism establishing or maintaining its own autonomy. Something very important

is also happening to the child, for he is learning that some of 'his play things' can *never* be internalized or made subject to his rational control. In his attitude to these 'objects', reasoning and instrumental thinking will continue to play some part, but *it is largely in the realm of feeling that such relationships will grow and be sustained.* In so far as the relationship cannot become rational and instrumental, it can only be spoken of in symbolic terms. We begin to see here the profound distinction which Martin Buber developed, between the categories of I/it—instrumentality and I/thou—relating to and learning through some person or symbol. As a general principle we can say that *felt meanings precede rational meanings.*

The play objects which resist instrumental assimilation are those bits of a child's environment which are most likely to retain and develop capacity for symbolic meaning. They denote in short what may be loved but what is hard to get. It is not merely parents or pets or friends who sometimes fill symbolic functions. Children can be much drawn to pictures, to natural scenes, buildings, music, which fill them with an oceanic sense of yearning and with intimations of distant beauty and significance. Given the right emotional atmosphere a child can be deeply stirred, for example, by readings from the scriptures or from poetry which are, in terms of developmental psychology, far ahead of his capacity to make rational sense of them. Indeed it is of the nature of myth, poetry and of much literature and art that we never do more than partially internalize their logical structure. Meanings which cannot be structured internally remain in the realm of feeling. This is why each repetition of an encounter with great art can provide new experience, a further, but never a final, move in the internalizing process.

The distinction which has been drawn between objects or words possessing a predominantly instrumental function and others which retain a symbolic function has often been masked in educational discussion by use of the terms 'instrumental' and 'expressive'. I regard this as a bent construct. The word 'expressive' in this polarity warps our understanding of the area where know- ledge and skill interact with feelings and experience. The misunderstanding goes back, probably to the popularization of psychoanalytic ideas in the early twentieth century. Many notions about how children need to express them- selves have become popular and even the term 'expressive arts' has gained currency. When the term 'self-expression' emphasized the need for children to have more freedom in a tightly disciplined society, it had value. But it now carries a certain lemon-squeezing connotation which suggests that riches and the light are within and merely have to be released.

SYMBOLIC MEANING

It is not, therefore, the 'expressive use' of words or pictures which should be seen as contrasting with instrumentality but rather their 'symbolic use'. This immediately brings us to the problem of how the word 'symbolic' should be understood. Following Freud and Jung to some extent, but more particularly Cassirer and Langer, I shall use it to refer to any sign which points to powerful but still obscure meanings, that is, to parts of language or other sign systems which are being employed in an exploratory way. The word originated as referring to two parts of a broken potsherd which when 'thrown' together gave a clue to someone's concealed or uncertain identity—a kind of password. But Piaget and some others, use it as referring to a sign having some resemblance to particular objects or events as, for instance, most road signs and some onomatopeic words.

The idea that the more significant use of language takes place in relatively 'rough ground', where there are considerable elements of doubt and ambiguity, links up with our notion (Chapter 4) of negotiated meanings and with William James' reference to the shadow areas surrounding words. George Herbert Mead was developing this idea in the nineteen twenties and his approach to social psychology, which became known as 'symbolic interactionism', is gaining ground once again in contemporary sociology. 'Symbolization' Mead writes, 'constitutes objects not constituted before, objects which would not exist except for the context of social relationships wherein symbolization occurs'. Notice that Mead is using 'objects' in a mentalistic sense where, perhaps, we might say 'concepts'. He continues: ... 'Meaning is thus not to be conceived, fundamentally, as a state of consciousness ... outside the field of experience [but] on the contrary, it should be conceived objectively, as having its existence entirely within this field'.[5] So, in terms of the present book, symbols are what we work with—arguing, testing, stretching meanings a little, as we move on and near frontier and away from the field of undifferentiated play. By contrast, in the other direction—towards greater control—we may be learning something by heart, writing a précis, playing a rule-governed game, practising a scale or giving an order. We are then moving away from pure play in the direction of increased competence in the individual and of efficiency in the group; but not in the direction of the enlargement of meaning.

This distinction is often obscured in practice because our different ways of learning overlap and succeed each other. But anyone concerned with education should be aware of the difference. It is, for example, in the direction of instrumentality that there is great scope for mechanization of learning, for here competence motivation is strong, fears are few, and the problems of error in self-evaluation are not great. In the other direction, however, the direction of discovery towards the learner's frontier, a teacher must be in close touch with the situation. The teacher's understanding of a developing emotional atmosphere, his greater knowledge of the abilities of children and of the structure of the subject, enable him to pose a question, to wait, to judge or to encourage, at the right moment and in the right atmosphere. It is largely because so much television education can only move a little way in this direction that its success has been so slight. Children's viewing tends to remain in the realm of undifferentiated and passive play, except when parents or teachers are there to enhance it, to push it in the direction of greater meaning.[6]

Within the relatively safe field of education, play can now be seen as becoming serious in two opposite, complementary directions: towards increasing the learner's competence and towards pushing out his frontier. Without participation of parents or teachers neither development would go very far.

NOTES

1. *Personal Knowledge*, p. 59.
2. A parallel discussion of similar ideas can be found in Karl Popper's essay 'The two Faces of Common Sense' in his *Objective Knowledge* (O.U.P., 1972). See especially sections 18, 19 and 20. Popper uses the term 'dispositional knowledge' to describe competence in an organism which is ready to learn.
3. *Playing and Reality* (Tavistock Publications, London, 1971), p. 96.
4. Bannister, D. and Fransella, Fay, *Inquiring Man* (Penguin Books, Harmondsworth, 1971), p. 19. For a critique of the neo-behaviourst view of socialization—'that the child is mere putty to be worked on by external "forces"'. See Martin Richards (ed.) in his introduction to *The Integration of a Child into a Social World* (C.U.P., 1974), pp. 4–8.
5. Mead, G. H. *Mind, Self and Society* (University of Chicago Press, 1962, (1934)), p. 78.
6. Some of the ideas in this and subsequent chapters are discussed in *Media and Symbols: the forms of expression, communication and education.* Ed. David R. Olson (University of Chicago Press, 1974). Chapter 3, 'Modes of Communication and the Acquisition of Symbolic Competence' by Larry Gross is particularly recommended. His terminology, however, is not coincident with mine in a number of respects. I came across the book only as the present volume was going to press.

CHAPTER 9

Systems

The higher organisms have sensitive skins, responsive nervous systems, and often an instinct which impels them, in play or in curiosity, to bring more variety into the system than is immediately necessary.

W. R. Ashby, *Introduction to Cybernetics*[1]

The two chapters which follow, on system and structure, are elementary but also speculative. In terms of the massive literature on both subjects they are much simplified, attempting only to point to concepts and perspectives which some readers may wish to investigate further. There is however a further speculative element in each which is concerned with the way in which teachers and learners often have the experience of being inside very complex systems, as opposed to being outside and controlling them. These ideas have a special relevance to educational theory but they should be recognized as not being well supported by other literature as is systems theory or, to a lesser extent, structuralism.

If the idea of instruction is to be rehabilitated as a central element in educational theory we need to understand better what structure is. But it has recently been emphasized that the concept of structure is not susceptible of clear understanding unless it is lodged in the more general concept of system.[2] For example a building is a man-made system within which a structural pattern of lines of tension and compression can be imagined; a sonnet is a linguistic organization, a sub-system of the great system of language, which has its own characteristic structure of rhythm and rhyme. General systems theory is concerned with these things but it has developed mainly as an effort to understand the complex organization of living, creatures and social systems.[3]

Language, like life itself, is a generative system. This means that though many aspects of the activity of speech or growth are rule-governed, they are nevertheless capable of developing in a diversity of activity and pattern to which there is no limit. General systems theory is interested in all aspects of organization and a body of theoretical knowledge has been developed which includes within its scope culture and social systems as well as biological ones, and it relates these to fundamental knowledge about energy, matter and information.

In Chapter 6 we discussed play in terms which can now be seen as being concerned with the adjustment of systems of different complexity to each other. The concepts of competence and frontier were then sketched and these can be regarded as being characteristic of the developing edge of a living or a cultural system. When we come to try to fit education into this way of thinking we shall have to consider the relationship of one mature human organism and one immature human or learner. Potential space is created between them by interplay. This field of play becomes culturally shaped and stretched so that it may develop 'serious' aspects. One of these aspects, which is directed towards a learner's competence is to do with perfecting skills, and the other, which is directed towards his frontier, is to do with discovery. Anticipating later chapters, therefore, we could say that play itself becomes organized into a system-like process which *is* education. But before following this up we must return to systems themselves.

A SYSTEM AT THE MECHANICAL LEVEL

If a teacher looks at his school in a rational, planning frame of mind he can usefully analyse its organization, functionally, on the following lines. Each sub-section can itself be divided in many different ways and the process of sub-division could be carried on many stages further as one proceeds to analyse the function of the different parts, first in biological, then in chemical terms. But if the analyst continues to sub-divide and identify functions of these parts in a school, the tree-like plan will tend to become both difficult and interesting at about the same time; when it becomes necessary to draw serpentine lines to indicate, for example, that a house master is also deputy careers counsellor and secretary to the Parents' Association. One of the characteristics of organic and of all the more complex systems now becomes apparent, that sub-systems generally perform several different functions. In a machine or in a factory assembly line 'the parts' are usually designed for only one, or very few, functions.

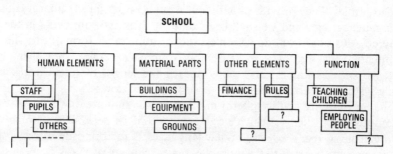

Figure 3. A system at the mechanical level

Mechanical systems are different from organic ones in other ways.[4] In manufacturing a car, designers and production engineers will plan production partly in terms of components, sub-assemblies and assemblies arranged in a simple functional tree. There are important lower (less complex) and upper limits to what has been allowed for in such a man-made hierarchy. At the lower limit, to take an example, the metal of a spring may be liable to crystallize (fatigue) after 10,000 hours of running—something that the designers may not have known about. At the upper limit the context in which the machine is used may change unforeseeably. A new speed limit may be imposed or the price of fuel may double. In the first instance we see that certain negative powers of the materials—liabilities if we use Harré's term—will always lie beyond the frontier of available knowledge. They will have to be allowed for, guessed about, but cannot always be fully understood. At the upper end, the larger context in which the system operates may change. Here the user will have to employ a degree of tolerance in the regulation of the machine, in what he expects of it and in shaping the context of its use.

All machines are designed with such elements of tolerance to cope with the unforeseen at both upper and lower limits. But machines differ markedly at these limits from living organisms. At the lower limit engineers try to ensure consistency of material and thus contain or control the powers (and liabilities) of the material. In living organisms there is no such cut-off and we find that the organs which constitute an animal contain tissues, which contain cells, which contain organelles, which contain ...... etc. At the upper limit the degree of play which organisms display to changing environment is great and is achieved in many ways which we generally call 'adaptation'. In cybernetic terms this involves an extensive movement of material and information in and out of the system. Such movement is, indeed, an aspect of the very nature of complex systems. 'That a System is *open*', writes Buckley, 'means not simply that it engages in interchanges with the environment, but that this interchange is an essential factor underlying the system's viability ... and its ability to change.'[5]

Living organisms are not the only open systems, though they are by far the most complex ones. Flames and meteorological phenomena, like storms, are also examples. They provide us with useful but very partial explanatory analogs of organic systems and we shall be examining them in more detail in the next chapter. All systems run down, unless fuel or some other form of orderliness is assimilated by them. The most obvious difference between non-living open systems, such as flames, and living ones is the length of time during which living systems are able to resist this tendency to run down.

The inevitability and long-term implications of running down are set out in thermodynamic theory, which need not concern us here, except to say that *entropy* can be regarded, in popular language, as the opposite of orderliness, similar in some respects to the more theological concept of chaos. Some systems, notably atoms and living organisms, have developed this capacity for holding off the running down process. Our own system of life has been going for about 2,000,000,000 years. Ervin Laszlo puts it this way:

> The living organism keeps itself in running condition as long as it can, and performs repairs if it gets damaged (these are the processes of healing and regeneration). But very complex organisms are unable to keep this

up indefinitely and succumb to internal exhaustion even when relatively undamaged (the process of aging). To survive, such species have managed to develop a way to perpetuate themselves by a form of super-repair: reproduction. Instead of replacing a damaged or worn-out part, they replace the entire organism. This way the individual organism undergoes the familiar life-cycle of birth, maturation and death, but in its course reproduces itself and thus keeps the species going. The individual now becomes like the ripple on the surface of a larger wave in the sea: the individual, like the ripple, is local and temporal, while the species, like the wave, is vast and ongoing. Yet all the ripples together define the curvature of the wave itself.[6]

I have gone a little way into this matter, partly in order to emphasize both the continuity and the extreme difference of degree between living and non-living system, but also because the notion that orderliness (neg-entropy, as Schrödinger called it) can be extracted from one substance and passed on to another represents, at the level of biochemistry, a useful analogy to the process of instruction.[7] It has already been emphasized that our thinking about education and about society in general is still too heavily influenced by mechanical and hydraulic (i.e. running down) models and the difference can now be seen in the context of the very wide framework of systems theory. Walter Buckley sums up the problem when he says that, sociological theory 'has been living for some time off the intellectual capital of previous centuries (and has been built) on mechanical and organic models . . . . . quite inappropriate in dealing with the type of system represented by the socio-cultural realm'.[8] Educational theory is not immune from this charge.

MORE COMPLEX SYSTEMS

There are some natural systems which, while near the frontier of science, may fairly soon be brought within its analytical domain. There are others, however, especially human ones, where bits of the system may be already explained, yet other parts or the larger 'wholes' within which men work appear to be very far from such explanatory treatment. As soon as we recognize that there is a system—a cell or a nebula for instance—we assume that there is in it a structure of related parts and this assumption puts the system, perhaps very remotely, in the realm of the explainable. We constantly have to cope with such systems which we are very far from being able to explain. The assumption of a 'scientifically educated man' is that most things—even all things—may be eventually explainable; but at the same time such a man will usually recognize, paradoxically perhaps, that most of his experience of nature and, a fortiori, of people, takes place at a level of complexity where understanding is to do with whole systems, not with parts, and with tendencies, directions and possibilities, not with mechanical explanations and control. An example of this tension between a rational man searching for explanatory structure and at the same time working within structures, is provided by Noam Chomsky. While on the one hand he has made great scientific advances in analysing the deep structure of language, he still *used* language to write, with a mixture of political opinion and passion, about the evils of the Vietnam war.

In the social sciences, provided that some organized systems can be discerned amongst all the complexity, it is reasonable to begin to look for the structural patterns or polarities which relate parts to wholes. Such structural relations may lead to modest predictions or to generalized interpretations, yet we may still retain quite a humble posture in face of the vastness of the whole system and of our partial understanding of it.[9]

LEVELS OF SYSTEM

One of the most puzzling experiences faced by teachers, especially those concerned with curricular innovation or teacher training, is the great difference that can exist between one learning situation and another. It might be thought that a well-trained teacher, bright children, good equipment and surroundings would necessarily add up to a successful teaching situation. But we know that often they do not. At other times, indeed, when circumstances may look much less favourable, something catalyses the mixture and all goes well. We may feel that there has been a distinct qualitative change but we are then hard put to it to explain or to predict such a situation. Phrases applicable to organic processes or to combustion do not, in such circumstances, seem out of place: 'the group seemed to catch fire' we say, 'the yeast was working', 'the concept jelled'. This is no accident for such processes *can* be understood in terms of living or open systems, when other analogies are inadequate. The interactions which we are trying to understand are of a complexity which cannot be comprehended in terms of one or two variables but only, if at all, in terms of probabilities and trends.

If such degrees of complexity are to be made accessible to understanding and to improvement, teachers, educational administrators and social psychologists need to become more familiar, not only with statistics, but also with the basic ideas which general systems theory provides.[10] There are two related concepts from this theoretical domain which seem particularly relevant to education and learning situations. These are:

(i) The three different levels of complexity at which systems work.
(ii) The idea of a directional field or pathway generated by systems, which we will touch on in the next section.

Living systems and some complex non-living and inorganic systems such as large meteorological processes or flames can function at three organizational levels: first, at the level of running down, like a guttering candle or like clockwork or like gradual death; or, secondly, they can function at a homeostatic level, with all systems more or less in balance, and examples would be a steady flame or sleep; or, thirdly, the system can spread dynamically, which we might associate with such spectacular phenomena as forest fires or burning newspapers. But dynamic burning is not necessarily violent and destructive. The flame in an internal combustion engine is disciplined by the piston and cylinders and the life of each flame, though brief, is under strict control, as it is initiated, mounts to a climax and is extinguished, in a rapid but smooth sequence. A growing tree and a child, an evolving species and life itself, can be considered a dynamic system of this sort.

So it is with the process of education, the tentative model which we shall suggest in Chapters 11 and 12 assumes that there is a dynamic system analogous to living or other systems in the interpersonal field of a teacher and a learner. It is not unduly fanciful to conceptualize such a field in terms of 'flame', for this calls to mind the highly developed and, for educational purposes, very necessary theories of system, structure and field. Nor is it unreasonable to extend Winnicott's 'potential space' to denote this field, which he identified in its simplest form. We would be wise, however, to refer such speculative terminology frequently to the realities they denote, namely, to a mother and an exploring child or to familiar classroom situations so that we may recall those real experiences which we know when, suddenly and encouragingly, a young living organism 'burns' with enthusiasm or interest. We would also be wise to bear in mind that in all the social sciences the use of these complex theories is in its infancy, and our models must be tentative.

PATHWAYS

Another concept from systems theory may now be briefly described as it offers explanatory possibilities which may help us to understand some of the social and cultural processes which are being discussed. I refer to the two similar concepts of pathways (or chreods) in the growth of living tissue and of 'equifinality'. These rather similar ideas are concerned with the directional development of processes by their interaction with other systems.

A very simple example of a pathway which has no channel and no goal is the Gulf Stream. Its flow and direction are the resultant of many winds and currents in the northern tropics and, indirectly, of the configuration of land and islands round the Caribbean. Some of the high altitude wind systems in the atmosphere offer even better examples for they do not even depend on the shape of the oceans and continents. The jet streams which flow very strongly at about 40,000 ft have no simple cause. They are the resultant of the world-wide system of thermal differences and of rotational movements on the globe's surface.

In embryology and in tissue regeneration in animals similar but even more remarkable phenomena have been commonly observed. For example, if a newt's leg is severed and if part of its tail is grafted on to the stump, a new leg and foot develop and not a misplaced tail. Someone brought up on old-fashioned notions of causality might have assumed that tail tissue contained in the nuclei of its cells special 'instructions' about becoming a tail. But not so. There *is* an immensely complex pattern of instructions in the DNA of every cell, but the form which a cell takes in 'obeying instructions' can vary very widely and depends on the context in which 'orders' are put into effect. It is necessary therefore to conceptualize a complex field of pressures, movements, gravitational pulls and chemical gradients, all of which contribute to the diverse forms which millions of cells will take as they assemble themselves into a new limb. C. H. Waddington explains why he invented the new term:

> Such systems usually exhibit a kind of stability. I have used the words canalization or homeorhesis to describe this. The latter is a new word. It is related to the well-known expression homeostasis, which is used in connection with systems which keep some variable at a stable value as time passes. A thermostat, for instance, is a device for producing homeostasis of temperature. We use the word homeorhesis when what is stabilized is not a constant value but is a particular course of change in time. If something happens to alter a homeorhetic system the control mechanisms do not bring it back to where it was at the time the alteration occurred, but bring it back to where it would normally have got to at some later time. The 'rhesis' part of the word is derived from the Greek word Rheo, to flow, and one can think of a homeorhetic system as rather like a stream running down the bottom of a valley, if a landslide occurs and pushes the stream off the valley bottom, it does not come back to the stream bed at the place where the diversion occurred, but some way farther down the slope. There seems to be no recognized word for a stabilized time trajectory of this kind. Since they are the most important features of developing biological systems, I have invented a name for them—the word chreod, derived from the Greek Chre, it is fated or necessary, and Hodos, a path.[11]

A somewhat similar notion in general systems theory with reference to educational systems is that of equifinality. Walter Buckley describes it in *Sociology and Modern Systems Theory* thus:

> The classical principle of causality held that similar conditions produce similar effects, and consequently dissimilar results are due to dissimilar conditions. Bertalanffy in analysing the self-regulating or morphostatic, features of open biological systems, loosened this classical conception by introducing the concept of 'equi-finality'. This holds that, in ontogenesis [i.e. individual development] . . . a final normal adult state may be reached by any number of developmental paths.[12]

These are instances, in biological and organizational terms, of what Freud in dream analysis and Louis Althusser in the study of political change call 'overdeterminedness' meaning not one, but very many causal influences pushing a complex system in a certain direction.[13] The end of such 'pathways' is *not* fixed; but it may be hard, nevertheless, to change.

What has all this to do with educational theory? Firstly, the whole idea of educational interaction is one which we may now hope to conceptualize more adequately in terms of general systems. Secondly, I would suggest that we would be justified in thinking of much individual learning as taking place *within* four-dimensional pathways analogous to the chreods or equifinal systems which we have been discussing. We learn, not in a vacuum nor in a mechanism but in a complex directional field.

When a child or an older learner or discoverer has a strong sense of meaning, long before he can attain a rational grasp of it, he can be seen as being within such a pathway. He cannot get outside the systems and so he comes to be aware of it through symbolic signs or rituals or through persons who carry symbolic meaning, who are also part of the field.

We are not confronted here with rival accounts of education but with complementary ones. Certain aspects of a child's education need to be understood in mechanical terms. He learns how an engine works or how to fill up a form or how to use a grammatical construction. These are processes in which a distinct mechanism is discernible. But if students and teachers are questioning or arguing or creating, especially in non-scientific subjects, they soon find themselves in problem areas where they cannot assume an entirely objective and instrumental position. With poetry for example, explanation gives place to interpretation and even this must be restrained. When we speak we are part of our own language system, of our own society and culture; yet by acknowledging this we do not reduce the importance and enjoyment of recognizing orderly patterns in literature. Similarly in a community: if I question a schoolboy's veracity, or if he questions mine, both of us are jointly concerned to clarify the formal structure of the system, called 'a school', of which we are mutually dependant members.

NOTES

1. *Op. Cit.* Chapter entitled 'Self-Regulation and Requisite Variety', pp. 208–18 (Wiley, New York, 1951) quoted by Emery, E. F., ed. *Systems Thinking* (Penguin Books, Harmondsworth, 1967), p. 117.
2. Boudon, R. *The Uses of Structuralism*, pp. 5–13 (Heinemann, London, 1971). For a history of the term 'structuralism' see Miriam Glucksmann, *Structural Analysis in Contemporary Social Thought*, Chapter 1 (Routledge and Kegan Paul, London, 1974).
3. Ludwig von Bertalanffy was the founder of modern systems theory. See his *General Systems Theory* (Braziller, New York, 1968). This synthesis was rooted in information theory and in cybernetics, see Norbert Wiener, *The Human Use of Human Beings: Cybernetics and Society* (Doubleday Anchor Books, New York, 1954).
4. Robert Persig's autobiographical novel *Zen and the Art of Motor Cycle Maintenance*, sub-title *An Enquiry into Values* (The Bodley Head, London, 1974) deals with systems and some other issues touching the theme of this book in an unconventional and not uncontroversial manner.
5. Buckley, W. *Sociology and Modern Systems Theory* (Prentice Hall, Inglewood Cliffs, 1967), p. 50.
6. *The Systems View of the World*, pp. 42–3 (Braziller, New York, 1972). This is a useful introduction to the whole field.
7. Schrödinger, E. *What is Life?* (C.U.P., 1944).
8. *Op. Cit.*, p. 1.

9. See Charles Taylor 'Interpretation and the Science of Man', *The Review of Metaphysics*, October 1971.
10. Some educational theory, especially that which relates to planning and administration, is still hampered by mechanical models. Michael MacDonald-Ross repudiates this when he writes 'The behavioural objectives approach to education rests in no sense whatsoever on any such systems theory. It simply relies upon systematic application of common sense to education. This is a worthwhile end in itself, and does not need the pretentious conceit so often found, where the mere linking of boxes by arrow is held to be sufficient justification for using the word "systems".' 'Behavioural Objectives A Critical Review', *Instructional Science* 2 (1973), pp. 1–52.
11. 'The Theory of Evolution Today', Koestler, A. and Smythies, J. R. eds. *Beyond Reductionism* (Hutchinson, London, 1969), p. 366.
12. *Op. Cit.*, p. 60.
13. For a further explanation see Miriam Glucksmann, *Structural Analysis in Contemporary Social Thought*, pp. 101, 147–8.

CHAPTER 10

Structure and the Curriculum

> What a representation offers in a confused and simultaneous form can be analysed and made available to the linear unwinding of language through an understanding of structure.
>
> Michael Foucault[1]

In Chapter 2 it was pointed out that posing a question presupposes a pattern or structure in which we discern an anomaly or loose end, and now we have seen that a structural way of thinking itself presupposes a system of some sort. In this chapter we shall take a closer look at the idea of structure, to see if it points the way to a deeper understanding of *instruction*. Our interest will be at the two main levels suggested in the previous chapter: the level at which structural concepts can be thought of as possibly leading to mechanistic or scientific explanations and the level at which a sense of structure helps us to correlate, interpret and enjoy phenomena without necessarily explaining them. We make hypotheses, which themselves are an elaborate form of question, when we see a sufficiently detailed structural network to lead us to believe that an explanation of the former kind *might* be attainable.

The subjunctive 'might' and 'if' of the hypothesis are very important. A scientist, Newton, for example, may reach a point in his enquiries where he sees that there *is* a further system to be investigated but he may also know that the time is not yet ripe for making further hypotheses. In science, Boudon observes 'the structural definitions may lag centuries behind the inductive definition'.[2] We are aware of relationships and structure long before we can explain them. In the arts too we may perceive structure and appreciate the whole patterned organization as a creative work. Yet when we enjoy a painting or a poem we do not wish and perhaps we are not able to go beyond perceiving that there are some pronounced structural relationships. As we noted in the parallel case of the therapist understanding the conflicts of a disturbed child (Chapter 4), to explain may be to do harm; but to interpret or to take part in the exploration of meaning may be a constructive response.

Many of the social sciences, and education too, are analogous in this to an applied art such as architecture. There is undoubtedly scope for analysis and for understanding structure but the approach through feeling, accompanying thought, is more important. If I look at the arches of Durham Cathedral I can become powerfully aware of the structural lines which are enshrouded in those massive, patterned stones—lines of force, of thrust and balance.

To know about such structure may deepen my appreciation of the whole but I do not have to evoke such knowledge consciously, any more than I need refer to grammatical terms as I speak or write.

In this chapter we shall consider structure first in its relation to our understanding of machines and then as it can be discerned in more complex natural and cultural systems. But first what *is* structure? James Moffett summed up the situation in his *Teaching the Universe of Discourse* where he points out that anything can be seen either as structure or a substance within a structure:

> If we presuppose that some things are structures and other things are substantive elements which go into structures, we have trapped ourselves at the outset. Everything is both, which is to say that things and relations are matters of conceptual opinion. To understand the option one is playing one must be aware of where one has mentally placed oneself. A tree is an element of a landscape, a thing, until we choose to isolate the tree, at which time it becomes a structure (if we talk about it at all) or set of relations among trunk, limbs and branches. By calling something a structure, we mean that we are preferring to strip it of context, in fact to make it itself the context for some smaller structures. A molecule is a structure of atoms, which are structures of smaller 'things', etc. A word is an element in a sentence, which is an element in a paragraph, which is an element in a composition.[3]

If we see a thing as a functioning whole we call it a system. If we even begin to analyse the working relationships of its parts we become conscious of structure. This may relate things in space, as in a building, or in time and space as in speech, or in an artistic performance as in music. There has been a considerable outpouring of structuralist literature especially in France and some of this is of dubious value. Boudon goes so far as to claim that it is only since the emergence of general systems theory that structuralist analysis can be regarded as having explanatory power. If this is so perhaps the time is now approaching when we can begin to use our understanding of structure to illuminate teaching problems and to guide educational practice.

We shall now consider three aspects of structuralist thinking which have special relevance to education:

(1) Generative rule-governed systems.
(2) The transformation of structure by instruction.
(3) Linear and multi-dimensional manifestations of structure.

The first is interesting but as its implications for education need a book to themselves we can only briefly indicate a connection between rules and structure and play. A living, evolving species is a generative system; so is mould in a cheese, or you eating it. So also is language, music or mathematics and so is a game of chess. But there is a difference between chess and the others. A game of chess is, for all its complexity, algorithmic, for the rule system of chess caters for all contingencies and does not change or have additional systems superimposed on it. Except in the pace of the game there is no slack in chess and it is a characteristic of men to enjoy playing within such tight systems. One would not concede either that the pieces on the board have intrinsic powers or that the system of rules by which they are moved can be modified during the game.[4] Rules are verbalized structures—verbalized either to bring about or to reflect consistency in relationships. I promulgate a rule to create order in this mob; or I formulate a rule to help me discover the order that was concealed within it. In living species and in some of the generative systems which emerge from them, expecially in languages, there is a degree of slack and of ambiguity which allows for the coexistence and interaction of various levels of rule-governed behaviour. Our main concern, however, is with structure in education and to this we must now turn.

INSTRUCTING

Let us consider a familiar learning situation, a child playing with building blocks, making a rather shaky construction and making discoveries at the same time. John is a six-year-old visitor and is playing with Dienes blocks, though not, as it happens, making arithmetical discoveries.[5] I had suggested that he build a tower and he decided to make it into a church; but he is not very adept and his construction now looks rather like Figure 4.

What are the sources and manifestations of structure here? From our window John could have seen a real tower and there is a church spire near his house; but he is not concerned at the moment with 'the real world'. He has the immediate problem of how to get one or two more blocks on top of the pile; and then the walls . . .

In adjusting the blocks so that they stay in balance John has been exploring,

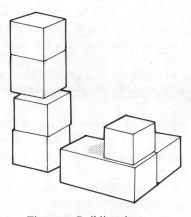

Figure 4. Building the tower

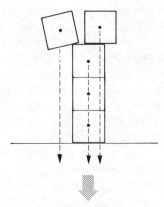

Figure 5. Diagram of the tower

in action, or *enactively*, the principles affecting the relation of the centres of gravity in a set of cubes. He does not know any of these terms and he has no abstract grasp of the task he is engaged on. But when he is about twelve years of age, he might, with a little help, be able to represent diagrammatically some of the principles involved. His *iconic* representation would then be something like Figure 5.

The terms *enactive* and *iconic* refer to two of the main prosthetic systems, by which we extend ourselves to control or understand the world. These are Bruner's terms and roughly represent 'learning by doing' and 'learning by pictures'.[6] At a further level of abstraction we also learn about and control the world by various sign systems such as language, algebra and musical notation which may be generally termed the semiotic mode. We shall see that enactive learning prepares for more abstract systems. But the more 'advanced' mode does not replace the earlier one; all three may be present and complement each other, even in original research.

Our concern now is with the structure which John has been exploring, enactively, as he built his tower. First of all we might consider some of the many routes by which this structural pattern has made its appearance on the table.

1. John has a capacity, innate, but improved by practice, to make guesses about his own perceptions and actions, and to test them. He does this while he builds.
2. He possesses, similarly, some degree of manual control, largely acquired.
3. He has seen towers of various kinds and can, we may suppose, recall these as mental images; though just how this is done and when the ability emerges, is still unknown.
4. He has learnt words to do with towers and buildings and they appear to have a double relationship with what he is doing: sometimes his efforts fill out the meaning of the word for him; sometimes the word may help

to initiate action. Edward Sapir refers to this function of language as 'the projection of potential meanings into the raw material of experience'.[7]

5. The blocks themselves are structured. They were designed and cut accurately as cubes and this makes them into a system capable of generating buildings or patterns or mathematical exercises.

6. I, the teacher, also took some part in the business. Having established a friendly relationship with my visitor I then produced the bricks, played with them for a minute or two and vaguely suggested 'towers'. I did this verbally and then enactively by putting two or three blocks on top of each other. Subsequently I made a few suggestions and encouraging noises.

7. The teacher also contributed an important, future-directed element by introducing mechanical and architectural questions which oriented the whole learning episode in an architectural direction, rather than in the narrower mathematical direction for which Dienes originally designed the blocks. The name which teachers give to educational 'subject matter' is not intrinsic to the playful activity of learning or even to the teaching materials in use. It derives, rather, from the long-range patterns of meaning by which teachers and others frame it, by their questions, hypotheses and assumptions. To the child 'play' is play; to the teacher it may also be the beginnings of a much wider business such as architecture.[8]

This is all fairly obvious, but the analysis contains most of the essentials of teaching/learning situations.

Numbers 1 and 2 represent John's initial competence for learning in an enactive mode.
Numbers 3 and 4 represent the first rudiments of higher level modes of learning—the iconic and semiotic.
Number 5 stands for the curriculum—all the selected and partially ordered stuff of learning situations.
Numbers 6 and 7. There is a teacher. He initiates the relationship, produces the material, suggests problematic goals and then watches and sustains the learning episode.

Structure became unified from these diverse sources by John's rather fumbling acts and 'entered' him. We say that he learnt something new, be became *in-structed*. Elements in the structure of the tower and some of the structure of the skill of building became part of his total neuro-muscular competence. These things come about mainly because John acted. It is not, I believe, overstating the case to say that all instructing and learning happen because of action by the learners. A child has to act on visual or auditory stimuli to make sense of them and thus starts to acquire perceptual skills when very young indeed. He has to act on toys, playing with them, to internalize a skill which is made accessible by them. Even the week-old infant makes hypotheses about his environment and eighteen months later he is making experimental patterns with language until he scores a success. Bruner writes:

> If you study the course of growth, you will discover that on a certain day, and it should be celebrated with an anniversary party each year, the child constructs a syntactical utterance. Mother washes jam from his hands. He says 'All gone sticky'.[9]

INSTRUCTING AND TRANSFORMING

Both these words in their original sense convey the idea we are discussing, that form (or structure) enters in. An important principle of structuralism follows from its concern with patterns rather than with things: the pattern can move on and leave the things behind. The bricks may be scattered but the building is remembered.

Consider music. A sonata is made—mysteriously—in a composer's brain. He hums bits of it and begins to write—not one—but several lines of notes on paper. This is later read by a pianist who converts it, via his piano, to sound waves. These then impinge on a microphone and are electronically transposed into a sequence of linear vibrations on tape. The music is then broadcast and goes out to a million ears. A few of the listeners remember the music and, again mysteriously, it has become internalized in their brains. In one respect the tape-recorder achieves greater abstraction than the musical notation. The score of a symphony may contain thirty variables at any one moment. The sound track reduces this to one—if it is not stereophonic. Some of these transformations are readily accessible to the explanatory analysis of science, others, as yet, are not. It may be many years, or never, before we have a clear picture of what actually happens in the inner structure of the brain at molecular or sub-molecular level, when you or I perform some simple act like 'inwardly humming a tune'.

Edmund Leach in his paper 'Structuralism and Social Anthropology' summarizes the situation when he remarks that it is 'perfectly clear that something must be common to all the forms through which the music has passed'. Then he gives us a definition:

> That common something is a patterning of internally organized relationships which I refer to by the word *structure*. It is the very essence of structures (in this sense) that they are capable of expression in multiple forms which are transformations of one another, and further ... there is no one particular form which is a *more* true or *more* correct expression of the underlying form than any other.[10]

Language too shows these properties of transformation even more clearly. As in music the manifestations of its structure can sometimes be envisaged as diffuse, spread out in a branching organization; at other times these structures are marshalled into a single linear form. Contrast, for example, the structure of a library with all its sections and sub-sections with the linear, sequential versions of the same organization—its decimal subject divisions, for example, or its alphabetical author catalogue. Or think of the language capacity of the scholar using the library. He is competent to handle twenty to thirty thousand words in an infinite variety of combinations and this competence resides mainly in the systematic networks of his brain. Even if he were gagged and bound in a padded cell he would still possess this. The existence of language in this diffuse, potential form is termed *langue* by linguists. But when our hypothetical scholar is free he may prepare to transform his ideas into articulate linear form After sitting for ten minutes he starts to write. Word after word 'flows' from his pen, sometimes easily sometimes laboriously. Or he whispers three sentences to a neighbour. Such utterances of language are known as *parole*—the linear or sequential performance of discursive writing or speech. But even though such *parole* is in a sequential string, it can still display a powerfully structured form by embedding one unit within a larger unit in a hierarchical structure. This is what grammar and phrasing do, or the sections and sub-sections of a book.[11]

The process of instruction is analogous to this transformation but it involves at least two people. We shall examine it more closely in Chapter 12. The structuring and transforming function of a teacher is the most central and positive aspect of education for it is he who prepares material, *suitably organized*, relevant, that is, to a learner's competence, and in an accessible, explorable form. But the word 'suitably' conceals an array of momentous questions. These are to do with the amount of slack that we leave in the system or with the manner and degree by which we make a complex idea concrete and consequently with the width of the channel suitable for its transmission. For example a complex scientific 'explanation' may be transformed into a fine articulate thread of argument with no asides or repetition and this may be scientifically excellent, in that it can then be readily shared by a community of like-minded experts and exposed to their detailed measurement and attempts at refutation; but it may be educationally useless. *The problem which faces an instructor is how to open up a compressed and often largely verbal model and make it accessible to the exploratory, untriggered energies of an x-year old.* Once this problem, which involves understanding both the structure of ideas and the developmental and assimilatory processes of children, has been approximately solved, then comes the other part of education which is about the child's readiness to explore novel experience or its need quietly to digest it.

An error of many progressives, swinging with tides of fashion, has been to overempahasize this permissive, letting be, aspect of our work, and a corresponding weakness of some recent English education has been our neglect of the formal side. A sterile debate is often carried on between so-called progressives and reactionaries, when what children are needing is new and more sensitively adapted structures in which to learn, in which even some old-fashioned things like team-work, perseverance and self-discipline may find their place, alongside discovery, play and enjoyment of the arts. A primary teacher in an Oxfordshire school told me how visitors from all over the world would arrive and watch, with enthusiastic awe, the free and purposive activity of her open-plan class. But she would usually find it necessary to explain how minutely structured it all was, what a close, yet scarcely visible, matrix of supplies, timing, expectation, habit and ritual had to be created, by her and by the children, before such 'free' learning could be sustained. We see again that freedom, like life itself and happiness, is, paradoxically, both the condition of, and the fruit of, certain high levels of organizaton and constraint.

This is partly a matter of teachers seeing into the children's interests and abilities. But unless a teacher himself has extensive mastery of the underlying patterns of ideas which he hopes the children will explore, he will not be in a position to know where they are likely to be able to ask interesting questions and find subsequent success. A teacher's knowledge should be as coherent as possible *for him;* but it should bristle with potential questions for his pupil. Instructing can now be seen as putting a learner in a position to transform his own representations of structure so that he may eventually, achieve 'the linear unwinding of language'.

COMPLEX STRUCTURES

There are, however, many tensions, conflicts and contradictions in a person's experience that cannot be transformed into rational and scientific thought. For a child most of his universe is in that category; for many adults, fortunately, there is a comforting area of rationality, which they keep trying, quite naturally, to extend. A scientist may have to make intuitive judgements about systems which still elude his hypothesizing. So also teachers, watching the enquiries of children, should be as interested in the processes of delay and in the holding

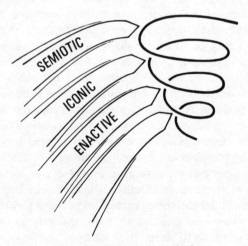

Figure 6. The spiral curriculum

open of some long term problems as they are in the speeding up of simpler problem solving.

To illustrate this at the level of classroom experience I shall describe a moderately complex system, considering it at the various levels of abstraction at which its structure is made manifest through teaching. This example, from physical geography, illustrates Bruner's idea that students may return to the same subject matter at different levels of abstraction. They discover more and more extensive structural patterns underlying phenomena as they move to more abstract conceptual levels; hence his well-known 'spiral curriculum' crudely represented in Figure 6. The arrows represent the main systems of representation by which we assimilate the structure of the world we experience. These are discussed in detail in the next chapter.

A geographer may have the experience of teaching about convection storms at several different age levels. At six a child may experience April showers and get a vivid sense of their gusty suddenness and of the possibility of hail and thunder. The child may run out, collect a lump of hail and dash for shelter. This is the stage at which Bruner's 'enactive' mode of coming to terms with new experience is in operation.

Teachers exploit such enactive responses as a major means for helping children to internalize experience. If a child asks about storms and hears them discussed by a teacher or parent he will also get the idea that there is more to it than this hail and this rushing in from the squall; that there may indeed be 'an explanation'. In terms of the language which he hears he is beginning to move beyond the enactive mode though his understanding and conceptual grasp is still at the level of what Piaget calls 'concrete operations', which as we shall see roughly parallels the period when iconic aids are likely to be most useful. The cultivation of a child's awareness of more to come, that there are complex explanations further along the road, and that he can have access to these whenever he wants to try, is a very important element in education. With an unconfident teacher there is a danger of this becoming a 'you're not old enough' gambit. But if handled properly such unripened seeds of interest may be powerful symbolic forerunners of subsequent exploration.

At the age of ten the same child may learn about convection currents and observe these in a glass trough of water over a Bunsen burner. This leads to his being given an acceptable explanation of April showers, namely that they are brought about by the differential heating of the earth's surface. This naive view is represented in Figure 7. But this is, from the meteorologist's point of view, a very inadequate account. Notice the relationship between the iconic model of the phenomena and the child's sense of 'explanation'. If he can manipulate a working model he is right to claim that he has an enactive explanation, even though he may not be able to explain the phenomenon verbally or even pictorially. Here again it is the teacher's task to leave a sense of understanding and also a sense that there is more to discover. At this stage too the teacher will be wise to establish some preliminary lateral associations with comparable moving air systems such as hurricanes or land and sea breezes.

Figure 7. Naive diagram of a convection storm

At sixteen the same complex mechanism of moving air masses needs to be approached at a higher conceptual level. Cross-sectional diagrams will now be inadequate. The iconic mode involving two and three dimensional models was appropriate to the last stage but must now be superseded by the more abstract and articulate semiotic mode. The life cycle of a convection storm will have to be imagined in time and in space, both on the large scale and at the microscopic scale of droplet formation. It becomes necessary to make the link with physics explicit and to understand how, in a convection cloud, latent heat from condensation is released in great quantities and to see how the storm becomes a 'thermal engine' run by this latent heat energy of damp air. In Piaget's terms this is 'a formal operation', an abstract mental handling of complex relationships. The student will also encounter the fascinating mechanism of hail formation which has been investigated in recent research for the Frontier of meteorology is not far away. The teacher may be asked about the generation of electricity in clouds and he may explain it by having recourse to further models—perhaps even to ones he knows are inadequate—like the static charges generated by friction, the rubbing of silk, etc. But here, once more, the conceptual structure should be left open for the physics specialist or for the inquisitive generalist to follow further if he wishes.[12]

There may be occasions when a student says to himself, quite rationally, 'I can see that I am not yet ready to understand this. I am prepared to wait till I am ready'. But such detachment must be exceptional. A far more likely reaction will be for the student to recognize his own perplexity and contain it in some partly rational and partly symbolic form until the time comes—if it ever does come—for the conflict to be resolved. I say 'if it ever comes' because there are many profound problems and conflicts which no student or scholar will ever fully understand and yet it may be very desirable that he be aware of them.

STRUCTURES OF THE CURRICULUM

When children study complex social systems it is more important that they enter imaginatively into the conflicts and doubts of human beings than that they acquire explanations. Indeed over-simple explanations can do considerable harm.

On a visit to a social studies class in a comprehensive school which is known for its work in this field, I talked with a fifteen-year old girl who was preparing a neat list which looked like this:

> Headmaster
> Deputy Head
> Housemaster
> etc. etc. etc.
> Jimmie Barnes
> The Cat

There were about a dozen items in the list and I was informed that this was 'The School's pecking order'. She had clearly got hold of an ethological concept on which perhaps it was hoped to build later. Nevertheless I could not help wondering if this activity might not have hindered her understanding of the real nature of the community of which she was a part. The head of this school was certainly not a dominating, authoritarian character. When I subsequently enquired about this I was told that the Sociology 'O' level paper 'required a knowledge of the vocabulary' of ethology and sociology! This example points to the kind of curriculum problem with which secondly schools are wrestling and for which we need more adequate theoretical understanding. We cannot examine the problem in detail but I would suggest that we would be wise to build social and humane studies around structures which in general are *not* explanatory but which can nevertheless lend coherence to the world we live in.

What sort of structural nodes and joints might give shape to a school's study of society? Jerome Bruner's *Man a Course of Study*[13] project was an attempt to answer this and it too used ethological and anthropological data. His central issues were the 'five great humanizing forces' of tool-making, language, social organization, the management of man's prolonged childhood and man's urge to explain the world; big themes for twelve-year olds but ones which were capable of *containing* subsidiary, ethological concepts like pecking orders or territory. These studies were set mainly in unsophisticated cultures which helped to keep the children at some distance from problems whose relevance to themselves they were left to discover. As this course is a good example of that still rare species—a concept-based and structure-based curriculum package— an outline of its main conceptual components is included as an appendix.

These few examples have been cited because a good deal of curricular development gets off to a false start because the theorists insist that a curriculum must be derived from or be aimed at things called 'objectives'. The word has become a shibboleth, as teachers who initiate reform without a suitably impressive list of objectives feel guilty or unprofessional. Fortunately, however, a few critics have already become restive about this. Lawrence Stenhouse, who is one of the most eloquent, writes as follows:

> Let us accept that education is concerned with disciplined activity in some broad sense. Then we may distinguish two forms of disciplined action, action disciplined by preconceived goals and action disciplined by principles of procedure. Thus to set out to learn eight guitar chords is to embark on a course of action disciplined by . . . . . a goal. On the other hand to write a sonnet is to hammer out a *part-formed intention in the framework of a* form.[14]

Stenhouse is making the extremely important point that in the second category form and structure should take priority when we plan a curriculum. Indeed most serious curricular development is of this second kind but far too often it is made to appear to be of the first kind.

Few people would deny that in practice it is sensible to identify specific objectives, or specific weaknesses that need remedying, and then to modify the curriculum accordingly. But as *an overall strategy we need to start with the intellectual framework of a subject and then to allow the learners to discover interesting ways in.* We can work out relevant starting points, or activities, or skill-training, at levels appropriate both to particular children and to whatever resources are available. Then may be the time to high-light objectives which individual children or groups can see.

THE RANGE OF STRUCTURES

There are some transcendent vistas of knowledge which lie beyond explanation but to which reference must be made. Examples would be—God, Nirvana, infinity, entropy. These are entities to which structure may be related, yet they cannot be included, or even approached, as explainable things. These metaphysical entities are capable of being symbolized but not of being comprehended. In an intermediate status, between such ineffable dimensions and the explanatory structures of the physical sciences, are many intermediate levels of structure of which we are commonly aware. I hesitate to write about this because there is so much work to be done by epistemologists and philosophers before we have an adequate basis for curriculum design.[15] Nevertheless in order to illustrate the kind of pragmatic structural thinking that *can* now be used in developing the curriculum and partly as a basis for discussion, I set out a tentative list as shown. This shows very approximately in order of abstraction, examples of the kind of structural elements that I have come across in discussing curricular problems with students and with colleagues.

If you ask a biologist of a geographer about the structures around which a secondary course might be designed you get a substantial list which will include many concepts of a 'process' kind like *nitrogen cycle* or *circulation of the*

ULTIMATES AND INFINITIES TRANSCENDING STRUCTURES	ENTROPY, GOD NIRVANA, INFINITY

STRUCTURES	EXAMPLES
Levels of orderliness	What makes men human? What is life?
Constructs	Powerful/weak, Good/evil, Beautiful/ugly
Performances	A wedding, an election
Processes	Evolution, The Renaissance, Conflict, Dialectic
Cycles	Nitrogen cycle, Carnot's engine,
Contextual concepts	Environment, field, space
Focusses	Town, a battle, a leader
Patterns	A sonnet, a matrix, perspective, counterpoint
Syntax and phraseology	An adverbial clause, A sentence
Taxonomies	Species, genus, phylum
Classifications	The periodic table, colours of the spectrum
Concrete concepts	Chairs, stars, people

PROPER NAMES	CHRIS'

STRUCTURES

Top and bottom entries are isolated because they are limiting cases which are not therefore relationships. They are, however, potential *relata*, i.e. that to which a structure can relate.

oceans, or they may be contextual concepts like *niche or environment*. With these there is usually some explanatory intention in the background. If however you ask a historian what would be examples of key structures or concepts around which secondary history courses are built you will probably get a less substantial answer.[16] The concept of *sovereignty* or some other large political idea might be offered or possibly some small scale process like 'the manorial system'. But in general historians do not like the assumption that explanatory models may be an important ingredient in their discipline. Instead they emphasize methods of enquiry, weighing evidence or cultivating imaginative powers as their teaching objectives. These are all important, but they are not an answer to the question about structures in school history.

Perhaps we have been looking for the wrong kind of structure. Raymond Boudon's ideas are helpful here: he suggests that we may often be able to identify a system and then identify structures in it while we are still a long way from assembling these structures into an explanatory model.[17] When we study human societies past or present, this is the stage we are at. Perhaps, indeed, this is the stage we will always be at; though, out of deference to the more Cartesian social scientists, this can be left an open question. The structural patterns that we look for in society are therefore not little, explanatory models but conflicts of interest, of purpose, power and ideal, the interactions of old and new technologies and the focusing of all these conflicts in unusual men and women. Here we have great tensions criss-crossing through groups and individuals. If a young historian can use his reason and intuition to imagine something of what it felt like to be Wellington or Wilberforce, a slave or a sufragette, to sense the complexity of their thought and feelings and the humanity of such individuals or types, that must surely be much more worth while than learning quasi-scientific explanations. Such imaginative work, however, needs to be lodged in a context of dates and events and it can endow these with warmth and colour.

A colleague and I were studying the pictures in school history books and the reactions of children to these.[18] It became evident that many of the most effective pictures were built up partly round constructs of the Kelly type— powerful/weak, loyal/treacherous, progressive/reactionary, etc.—there is an interesting field of enquiry here and a promising empirical technique to be developed: to what extent are history and social studies influencing children's personal constructs? To what extent is this being done in crude good-man/bad-man terms and to what extent are more refined constructs being developed? We do not know nearly enough about this, yet it is in those parts of the school curriculum where structures are open, where children deploy their own evaluative constructs, that most can be done for moral education.

A teacher trying out new materials or a curriculum design team working on a larger project will be wise to bring the structures which give coherence to their own knowledge to the forefront of their minds; but it is not their business to make such structure explicit. The practical and outward task of a curriculum planner is to do with the activities and skills, enjoyment and discoveries of potential students.

The curriculum is a small world or microculture created by teachers at various levels of abstraction for learners to explore. In such exploration, not only will some of the structure of knowledge be rediscovered, but values will also be kindled, for *it is only in creative and open situations that the learner's own evaluative powers and judgement are brought into play.* Because these situations are unlikely to be created or long sustained by learners working on their own, the quality of teachers and teaching becomes paramount.

The distinction between a syllabus and a curriculum can now be made clear and we need to see these terms as extreme points on a continuum. A syllabus is a linear arrangement of testable items; a curriculum is a complex branching structure, a cultural artefact made by teachers. A curriculum should be designed so that it can be explored, yet continually modified, in order to maximize the development of a learner's skills and the extension of his conceptual control. The lower branches of a real curriculum (as opposed to the theoretical one defined above) do contain chunks of linear material and *cul-de-sacs* and favoured domains and biasses. To some extent the exploration of these lower branches is testable and predictable. But in its higher stages an effective, open curriculum runs up towards the frontiers of human creativity and of original discovery. At these levels, though the general style of an art or a science may be specifiable, unpredictability and untestability should be expected.

Every educational situation has two faces: that seen by the child, where structures are obscure and purposes are oblique, where feelings predominate over clear thinking and where short-term objectives—lunch for example— readily supervene; and there is the face seen by the adult, where principles and structures are less obscure and longer-term objectives—like G.C.E. 'A' levels or the ability to weigh evidence—seem obviously desirable. The art of teaching is to see both, to relate them and go beyond them.

NOTES

1. From p. 148 in *Les Mots et Les Choses*. The above, slightly free translation, gives the meaning better than that which appears in the English version of the book *The Structure of Things* (Tavistock, Publications, London, 1970), p. 136.
2. Boudon, R. *The Uses of Structuralism* (Heinemann, London, 1971, Paris, 1968).
3. *Op. Cit.* Moffett, James (Houghton Mifflin, Boston, 1968), p. 2.
4. This distinction may be drawn too sharply. In the higher levels of chess-playing new principles may become apparent which, when acknowledged, take on some of the characteristics of rules, or at least, of conventions. An algorithmic system may therefore display emergent properties without being open to the intrusion of new systems from outside.
5. See Z. P. Dienes, *Building up mathematics* (Hutchinson, London, 1960) and other works by him.
6. Though Bruner's scheme can be criticized and usefully modified (Chapter 11), the iconic mode is a particularly useful concept, for we *do* constantly think with pictures, both internally and externally. But the problem of music remains: is it a mode on its own or a special version of the iconic?
7. *Culture, Language and Personality* (University of California Press, 1949). Vygotsky too in *Thought of Language* (M. I. T. 1962) emphasizes the way in which language leads the way in cognitive development.
8. This is an important point which cannot be followed up in the present book, but it suggests a way of dealing with the problem of how we formalize knowledge, more promising than those currently fashionable in education. (See Chapter 3, above). We probably need to see school subjects as being shaped by the joint influence of innovators working at the Frontiers of knowledge *and* of teachers who formulate questions appropriate to a particular learning stage.
9. *Toward a Theory of Instruction*, p. 104. Enquiry in psycho-linguistics has paid much attention to phrases like this and a category of *pivotal* pre-grammatical words like 'all-gone' has been identified and another *open* category. See David MacNeills paper in *The Genesis of Language* (M. I. T., 1966) eds. George A. Miller and Frank Smith.
10. In *Structuralism: An Introduction*, Wolfson College Lectures 1972. ed. Robey, D. (O. U. P., 1973). The example of a work of music is used by Leach and ascribed to Bertrand Russell.
11. For example: on p. 441 of Toynbee's *Study of History*, Vol. I, there is an 'additional note' to sub-sub-section (2) of sub-section (a) of Section II of Sub-Part C of Part II of the whole work. Is this a record?
12. The story of how the scientific study of clouds, started with Luke Howard F.R.S. in 1802. He influenced and was influenced by the observation of artists, including Goethe. See Kurt Bedt's *John Constable's Clouds* (Routledge as Kegan Paul, London, 1950) But attention to the detailed understanding of how clouds function had to wait for 150 years: an example of lag between the recognition of a system and the elucidation of its structure.
13. Chapter 4 in *Toward a Theory of Instruction*, describes the ideas behind this important project. M. A. C. O. S. was the work of a team of scholars of which Bruner was a

leading member. The Centre of Advanced Research in Education at the University of East Anglia has a unit concerned with this material.

14. Lawrence Stenhouse, 'Some Limitations to the Use of Objectives in Curriculum Research and Planning'. *Paedagogica Europaea* 1970/71. (My italics) For another example, Hugh Sockett 'Bloom's Taxonomy: A Philosophical Critique'. *Cambridge Journal of Education*, Vol. I, 1971. But the most powerful criticism is in MacDonald Ross' paper 'Behavioural Objective—A Critical Review' cited in the notes on the preceding chapter.

15. An important book, pointing in this direction, is J. L. Jolley's *The Fabric of Knowledge* (Duckworth, London, 1974) which sets out a fundamental, allegedly culture-free, system which may be of value in clarifying these problems.

16. Coultham, J. B. in *The Development of Thinking and the Learning of History* (The Historical Association).

17. Boudon, R. *Op*. Cit., Chapter I.

18. Warr, A. D. Unpublished work on the effect of visual aids on teaching style.

Part Three

Possible Models

CHAPTER 11

The Four Modes of Instruction

To know an object is to act upon it and to transform it.

Jean Piaget[1]

Mental growth is not a gradual accretion, either of association or of stimulus response connections ... [but is] much more like a staircase with rather sharp rises, more a matter of spurts and rests.

Jerome S. Bruner[2]

Jean Piaget has been the mentor of teachers for fifty years and many of his most important insights have already influenced our schools. Perhaps the most notable result of his early work came in the 1930s when people like Susan and Nathan Isaacs began to disseminate his ideas so that they spread, through the British Colleges of Education, to many primary schools. No less striking has been Piaget's profound influence on the curriculum reforms of the nineteen sixties, especially in mathematics and in science. In the pages which follow I shall refer to a few areas where criticisms have been made of the generally received Piagetian doctrine. But I am using, not disputing, his central descriptive and conceptual scheme. It is important that this developmental theory should be seen as being open to modification and criticism, for the most serious danger which threatens the work of any original thinker is that of becoming static or dogmatic.

Perhaps Piaget's most fundamental insight has been his understanding of the positive and creative nature of all learning. His has been the voice which, of all others, should have eliminated from our teaching the dreary assumptions of the bucket theory—of 'getting something into the children's heads'. But success still seems far away, partly because of the narrowly rationalistic way in which we tend to view education, but also because of the enormous quantitative and selective pressures operating in national systems. In a recent book Piaget returns to the theme and stresses that 'the essential functions of intelligence consist in understanding and inventing, in other words, in building up structures by structuring reality.'[3] He goes on to point out that understanding is subordinate to invention and that the problem of intelligence is thus limited to a 'fundamental epistemological problem of the nature of knowledge'. And then he puts the key question: 'Does the latter constitute a copy of reality or, on the contrary, is it an assimilation of reality into a structure of transformations?'[4] Piaget's answer is, not surprisingly, the second; but to get the impact of this it is necessary to recall the emphasis which the structuralists place on the notion that no one version of a structure has priority over the others. The way Piaget puts it, therefore, is not to suggest that we are receptacles or collectors of impressions, not that we are all-powerful shapers of a plastic world, but rather that all our mental creations reflect the patterns which lie outside us in nature and in peoples minds; that there is, in effect, a dialectical process at work harmonising internal mental patterns and external ones, and that this harmony is, in part, our own making.

Around this basic orientation there are three elements in Piaget's psychological system which call for special note. There is his experimental procedure, which has been criticized for its narrowness and lack of rigour; it is, however, being improved and modified by numerous child psychologists all over the world and they are consolidating and modifying his findings. Then there is Piaget's main developmental 'stair-case' and its related terminology. Here there are already criticisms about the position of some of the steps or 'risers' and the suggestion being made that their order may be less inevitable than Piaget has sometimes maintained.[5] The third element of Piaget's work which offers something to a theory of education is his dialectical approach. He believes that we enlarge our stock of knowledge, sometimes by assimilating new experiences to an existing mental pattern or schema and sometimes, when the schema itself is inadequate, we follow a more radical procedure and have to change our own patterns, or in his terms, to accommodate our schemas in order to internalize an unfamiliar structure. Accommodation comes at the point on our journey when we stop trying to cram souvenirs into our old luggage and buy a new suit-case. It has been pointed out that the first process—assimilation—involves us in adjusting the world to our picture; and the second involves us in adapting our mental schemas to the world, and it is then *we* who change. These distinctions have been criticized as being somewhat naive but their usefulness is increased when it is realized that the assimilation/accommodation distinction is not absolute; there are intermediate degrees of adjustment.

I have proposed that we use the word 'frontier' for the zone in which personal discoveries are made and this now becomes relevant. In so far as accommodatory learning is taking place—even if only in small degree—a child is pushing back his frontier—making his own discoveries. It would be hard on pupils to assume that education must be a process of continual stretch and the need for considerable periods of rest and play and practice is emphasized by Bruner in the quotation at the head of this chapter. Nevertheless the reality of the learning frontier, a zone of potentially disturbing questions, which bounds every learning situation, is something of which all teachers must be conscious. Children's awareness of this frontier will be less explicit and clear; they will *feel* it. They rarely express such feelings in words but their faces and actions are eloquent. Their interest, curiosity, excitement—fear too perhaps—will be evident and their efforts may be sustained for more than the normal brief spasms.

Piaget's main task has been descriptive, to let us see how children think; Bruner, in his *Toward a Theory of Instruction*, sketched out a prescriptive theory and stressed the need for developing a programme, backed up by empirical observation, which would tell us *what to do* in order to assist learning. In the rest of this chapter I propose to lay Piaget's developmental ideas and Bruner's prescriptive suggestions alongside each other and to develop the latter in one or two respects.

FOUR MODES OF REPRESENTING REALITY WHICH FACILITATE LEARNING

In *Toward a Theory of Instruction* Bruner accepts Piaget's general descriptive accounts of children's development and acknowledges him as a great epistemologist. But he is critical of some aspects of his psychological theories, such as those explanations of learning in terms of an oscillation between accommodation and assimilation which we have just mentioned. Bruner regards these as being too 'easy', 'a portmanteau theory' which 'in no sense constitute[s] an explanation or psychological description of the processes of growth'. He concludes his essay 'Patterns of Growth' with this summary of the task which lies ahead of educational psychologists:

> ... the heart of the educational process consists in providing *aids and dialogues for translating experience into more powerful systems of notation and ordering.* And it is for this reason that I think a theory of development must be linked both to a theory of knowledge and to a theory of instruction, or be doomed to triviality.[6]

Earlier in this essay Bruner has given us what appear to be essential elements for a theory of instruction and it is these that will have to be integrated into a wider theory of education. Bruner asks how a child uses, or is helped to use, representations of its world to 'get free of present stimuli and to conserve past experience in a model'. He refers to 'the rules that govern storage and retrieval from this model', and goes on to suggest that three modes of representation are available to promote these processes.

> Much of our research has been directed at the elucidation of this matter. What is meant by representation? What does it mean to translate experience into a model of the world? Let me suggest that there are probably three ways in which human beings accomplish this feat. The first is through action. We know many things for which we have no imagery and no words, and they are very hard to teach to anybody by the use of words or diagrams and pictures. If you have tried to coach somebody at tennis or skiing or to teach a child to ride a bike, you will have been struck by the wordlessness and the diagrammatic impotence of the process. ... There is a second system of representation that depends on visual and other sensory organi-

zation and upon the use of summarizing images. ... We have come to talk about the first form of representation as *enactive* and the second as *iconic*......

Finally, there is representation in words and language. Its hallmark is that it is *symbolic* in nature, with certain features of symbolic systems that are only now coming to be understood. Symbols (words) are arbitrary, ... they are remote in reference and they are almost always highly productive or generative in the sense that a language or any symbol system has rules for the formation and transformation of sentences that can turn reality over on its beam ends beyond what is possible through actions or images. [7]

These are important ideas but there are two points on which I think Bruner's scheme needs to be qualified. One, to which I have already referred, is that he uses 'symbolic' where it is liable to create problems of meaning and where a term like 'linguistic', 'semiotic' or 'articulate' would be more suitable. The second qualification, one which we shall return to later, is that Bruner does not elaborate the fundamental mode of initial learning through which an infant first makes sense of his experiences—*through other people*—especially its mother. This may be termed 'interpersonal'. I propose therefore to modify Bruner's scheme and classify four modes of instruction as follows:

The interpersonal mode	—mainly, at first, through the mother.
The enactive mode	—through autonomous action.
The iconic mode	—through images and models which are mainly visual.
The semiotic mode	—having reference to signs which are potentially part of a coded linguistic system. [8,9]

A semantic problem should be faced at this point about the word 'representation'. Do these modes refer to mental operations or to external events and things? The answer is 'both'. Undoubtedly we do acquire the ability to use words or pictures or actions internally. But the patterns in which they are embedded are largely external in origin and these are generally described in cultural terms, so the emphasis in this chapter will be on instructional *things* rather than on the mental operation of imagined things. But such distinctions should not obscure the fact that we are dealing with two aspects of a teaching/ learning process.

These four modes represent the main levels at which *children discover* or *are helped to discover* their world. 'Discover' implies the possibility of self-instruction: 'are helped to discover' implies a teacher's instruction. It is reasonable to call these the four modes of 'instruction' if we use the word in its wide sense, as each mode relates to action through parts of the body or sense organs or through external things or through signs derived from them—

all of which facilitate the internalizing of structure. Though the process of instruction is almost always initiated by an adult there is present the assumption, and hope, that it will lead to an autonomous learning process.

In the following quotation, John Shotter not only summarizes the nature of the first, interpersonal mode of instruction but he also touches on several ideas which have already been put forward in this book. He is commenting on a passage by R. Spitz on the significance and reciprocity of infants' smiling. Shotter writes:

> Although the relationship between a mother and her child is clearly un-equal, they do each have *the power in some sense to complete one another's* intentions. To the extent that a mother can appreciate the intentional structure in her baby's rudimentary movements, she can complete their intention and in some manner satisfy his needs for him. But the mother too pursues intentions within the interactive scheme. She wants her baby to suck, to stop crying, to acknowledge her by looking into her eyes, to grasp her finger, etc. And she discovers strategies and tactics via which she can 'elicit' these responses—she cannot, of course, elicit the whole pattern of response from the child as a pattern, he must already have the power to structure his activity so, and she simply discovers a way of making him manifest that power. The development of the ability to conduct such a structured reciprocal relationship as this is evidently a precursor to the later playing of games.
> Now within the totality of the child and his mother, the child's mother initially constitutes a 'mechanism' via which he can execute not move-ments but actions in the world. ... But no mother can appreciate the needs of her child perfectly, nor could she devote the whole of her life to him, even were she able to do so, there are moments when he must fend for himself. During those moments when she ceases to be *his* 'mechanism' she becomes simply an aspect of his environment to which he must adapt like any other. The interactive link within which mutual fulfilment of intentions takes place is severed. The child is initially nurtured within this link, but whether it is operative or not must be one of the very first distinctions he draws, and knowing how to establish it (or deny it) one of the first social skills he learns. In making the transition from a disorganized, syncretic link with his mother to a definite well-defined optional link, the child is developing from a natural agent to an individual personality.[10]

Shotter suggests that for about the first year of its life a child lives in this close 'symbiotic' relationship with its mother, but when it first learns to crawl it terminates this phase. In our terms one could say that the period when res-ponsiveness is the predominant mode of instruction is ended by the child's 'enactive' move away from its mother. From then on, and for several years, the enactive mode will predominate but the child will constantly regress to the interpersonal mode. Merleau-Ponty on a similar theme in *The Penomenology*

96

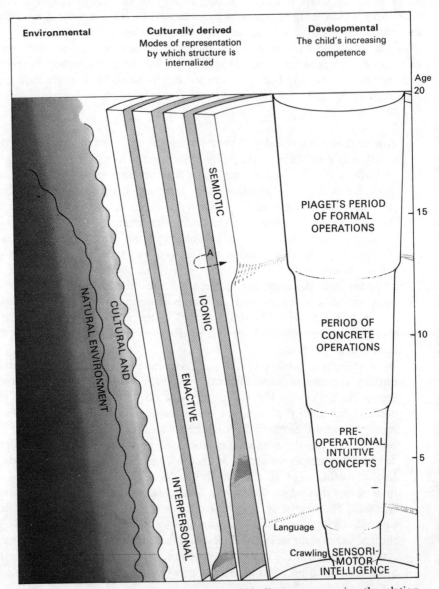

Figure 8. The four modes of representation. This diagram summarizes the relationship between the descriptive terminology of developmental psychology and the modes of instruction which make available increasingly abstract representations of the perceived world. The four central bands are highly schematized. The term 'semiotic' has been used in place of Bruner's 'symbolic' and it can be taken as denoting articulate, language-like systems of signs.

of Perception[11] describes this as follows in more adult terms: 'In the experience of dialogue there is constituted between the other person and myself a common ground; my thought and his are interwoven into a single fabric ... they are inserted into a shared operation of which neither of us is the creator ...' Even during the period of shotter's 'symbiotic relationship', when the interpersonal mode predominates, the other modes are being foreshadowed. Indeed these modes are in evidence almost from birth, for an infant acts, visualizes and vocalizes, and in all these we see the early forerunners of the three main subsequent modes of learning and teaching.

If Piaget's general developmental scheme and the extended version of Bruner's modes of instruction are set alongside, we can see how the two are complementary (Figure 8). It should be emphasized, however, that this diagrammatic analysis of instructional modes is only a crude and tentative outline. Piaget describes how a child progressively comes to make sense of the world and Bruner suggests how we, teachers, can enhance the process. The four modes refer to the kind of acts and 'prosthetic aids' or extensions to the person which an instructor helps to supply. These include all the culturally transmitted routines, games and toys, associated with enactive learning; all the pictures, maps, charts and diagrams associated with iconic learning; all the semiotic or sign systems of articulate language, mathematics and music which make abstract thinking possible. There is a certain shading of one mode into the next but they are sufficiently distinct to justify the four-fold classification. Shotter stresses the very limited range of accurate knowledge in this whole area and observes that 'the invention of games, clearly cries out for further research. Children reveal their powers in the games they play. *What* children can be inducted into *what* games and *what* age and *how* is not at present known in any detail' (note 12, p. 50 above). Similar comments could be made in regard to our understanding of the iconic aspect of instruction.

The psychological and pedagogical terminologies need to be kept distinct, even though they constantly interact. The psychological vocabulary is about processes of learning in a child and to the usual terminology we have added that of competence, in a rather special sense, and 'frontier'. The pedagogical vocabulary is about cultural things and acts with which adults create a field for learning. The frontier concept is common to both: to the learner it is an existential reality; to the teacher it is a useful conceptualization of the outer limits of a learner's system—something of which he needs to be very much aware. The first function of an educational theory should be to make us more conscious of the options we can move among. As we proceed from the more general to the more abstract in the field of instruction, from enactive to iconic for example, we are moving away from four-dimensional representation (as in ballet) to three or two-dimensional representations (models or maps), and we approach one-dimensional and linear forms in speech or writing. To be able to teach is to be able to move learning situations skilfully up and down this scale.

MOBILITY AMONG THE MODES OF INSTRUCTION

Figure 8 above attempts to sum up the way in which the stages of a child's education are characterized by the predominant modes of instruction. At any given stage, if a teacher and pupil run into difficulty what do they do? If the difficulty has been about algebraic notation the teacher will encourage the pupil to revert to an iconic expression of the same difficulty, to a graph perhaps. Such a manoeuvre is suggested at point 'A' on the diagram. If a child is having difficulty about the continuous curve of a graph he may be encouraged to remember how, a few years ago, he did histograms, moving around the class and measuring everyone's heights and putting them into an array of steps. If one mode proves too difficult, teacher and learner regress to a simpler and more concrete mode.

In looking at Figure 8 it would be wrong to suppose that the various steps or risers are fixed, for they will vary with individuals and with cultures. What is presented here, however, is a way of relating external representational and instructional systems to the internal development of mental powers. The chart shows for example that to a child between the ages of about seven and twelve the iconic mode of instruction and discovery is likely to be the most effective. It will be used together with, and be supported by, the enactive and interpersonal modes. With a disturbed child, or with a group in some kind of crisis, the teacher may have to reach back to the basic interpersonal relationship; but in normal situations he will be exploiting mainly the intructional possibilities of iconic representation and allowing autonomous learning to be dealt with more by enactive and interpersonal modes. One could put it another way by saying that at this stage the novel skills for which the teacher takes the initiative will be mainly ones with a marked iconic content and that these may be embedded in enactive situations.

Consider this example. Children playing freely with light and heavy objects will gain some idea of comparative weights, but if a simple beam balance is used, an iconic demonstration of proportionate weighing will be possible. The modes overlap and some aids are particularly useful in bringing about the transition from a less to a more abstract mode. A child's play with the balance could be properly termed 'enactive'; but the iconic message which the balance contributes is rich, for it relates levers, pivots, weight and proportion in one almost two-dimensional assembly.

Does this then mean that the more advanced semiotic, language-like mode can be neglected at this ten-year-old stage? Not at all. Speech and mathematical notations should not be in the forefront of the teacher's mind as he plans his teaching, but they still play a part by giving him confidence and intellectual mobility. Nor should advanced words be too scrupulously avoided. A child will have and use many intuitively acquired concepts from about four onwards and many of these will have verbal tags whose fuller meanings await development.

Piaget stresses that at the age of about eight many problems and concepts can be handled in concrete terms—'the operations ... are still applied solely to objects, not to hypotheses set out verbally in the form of propositions—hence the uselessness of lecturing to the younger classes in primary schools and the necessity of concentrating on concrete methods'.[12] A child of eight or ten will not have the capacity to handle words as heuristic devices—to turn such verbal forms around or to check their logic. It is this that Piaget means by formal operations—the handling of abstract forms. And it is this active manipulation of sign systems, as in algebra, in logic or in weighing evidence, which can begin to take precedence over iconic representations after the age of about twelve or thirteen. Speech works at various levels and though many of the more abstract connotations of adult words will be missed by a ten-year-old, many of them will, nevertheless, be taking root in his less abstract, concrete experience. In this way a 'powerful word' can often function as a symbol when it cannot be brought under rational control.

An interesting suggestion which relates the work of Bower and the ideas of Bruner which we have developed in this chapter, comes from Japan in the form of a personal communication about children's perception discussed by John M. Kennedy in his *A Psychology of Picture Perception*.[13] Sakuichi Nakagawa, who appears not to know of Bruner's work, lays more emphasis on the internal, mental operations than I have done. I stressed the cultural origin of the signs and shapes with which we teach; he stresses the process of thought which uses them. Kennedy explains Nakagawa's ideas:

> Children begin as four-dimensional perceivers. They register the 'events' of their environment, rather than all the static 'appearances' of objects. Later they become three-dimensional perceivers, detecting the shapes of objects. Still later they become capable of two-dimensional perception, capable of registering flat shapes or information provided by marks on flat surfaces. This Japanese view developed quite independently of Bower's work. Yet there is a fascinating parallel between Bower's findings and Nakagawa's theory. The crowning touch is that Bower finds that very young infants will not accept a static object as being equivalent to the same object in motion. An infant following a moving object with his eyes will not continue to look at the object when it comes to rest. Instead, he will continue his tracking motion briefly after the object stops, and then look around, for all the word as though he were trying to find a missing object. The stationary object is not 'recognized' .... as the heir to the moving object.[14]

> Nakagawa's ideas together with Bower's research suggest a three-step sequence: first, the young infant registers objects in motion and fails to connect a stationary object with the same object in motion. Second, the child recognizes objects that are static, like Bower's cubes, but not when depicted. Third, the infant, in a steadily maturing development of a capacity to recognize the same object in many guises, comes to recognise pictorial information, static information, and motion-carried information as being equivalent.

It is quite possible that in our print-dominated and spectator oriented culture we have neglected the *intellectual* value of the arts and of model-making, quite apart from their emotional value. It is a mistake to think the higher, abstract or linguistic statements are 'better'. For many purposes, besides teaching, the more concrete, multi-dimensional modes are more appropriate. They allow for more feeling, for more sense of freedom and open-ness and they can provide a favourable ethos for the making of discoveries.

Rom Harré argues in his *Principles of Scientific Thinking* that the iconic mode must sometimes be given priority over the semiotic mode. He has no doubt that language and mathematics have great importance in the checking of hypotheses, in the sharing of conclusions and in the generating of criticism. But he suggests that where original scientific work is being done, the mental model, and the discussion of it, have priority over the framing of 'laws', and over the mathematical or verbal descriptions of nature. Harré asks 'What are the vehicles of thought' in which original science is carried out? He discusses language and mathematics as well as pictures, models and diagrams. But he concludes 'that we actually operate with a complex of vehicles for thought, one ... outward manifestation of which I shall call a statement-picture complex typically consisting of a working drawing and a statement of how the structure depicted will react to appropriate stimuli. We cannot fully understand the way sentences function ... if they are considered in isolation from the statement-picture complex to which they belong.'[15] Creative work, like education, often starts with interpersonal enactive and iconic initiatives. It can then be communicated, criticized and compressed in the semiotic mode.

I doubt if, either in science, in the arts or in education, we have more than a faint idea about how these modes of representation and instruction depend on each other and interact. The relationship of this hierarchical way of looking at the instructional process to Kohlberg's parallel hierarchy of moral educational stages also needs closer examination than is possible here.[16] In terms of practical experience and of the many-sidedness of teaching, the following generalization is offered.

As a manager of learning situations a teacher will try to get as much of the work as possible done by the children in a free autonomous play-like situation using the modes of instruction they have already mastered. In the case of our ten-year-old this would be in active behaviour and in interpersonal (social) behaviour.

As an instructor, introducing new structures, a teacher will be largely concerned to provide opportunities for children to work and have experiences in the most abstract mode of which they are capable. In our ten-year-old example this would be at the iconic level.

As a therapist the teacher will have mastery of the arts of regression, that is of allowing children to handle the same subject matter at less abstract levels and so to strengthen any weaknesses in their foundations of competence, their feelings of being able to cope.

A teacher also has what might be termed a prophetic function. He can sometimes help a child to hook on to symbolic representations of the world which are shadowy at the moment of apprehension but which, years after, may fit into a clearer and more comprehensive pattern. Or they may never do so; some shadows, including our own, are always with us.

NOTES

1. *Science of Education and the Psychology of the Child* (Longman, London, 1971), p. 29. In this Chapter I shall only give brief explanations of Piaget's terminology and developmental system.
2. *Toward a Theory of Instruction*, 'Education as Social Invention' (W. W. Norton, New York, 1968), p. 27.
3. *Op. Cit.*, p. 27.
4. *Op. Cit.*, p. 28.
5. One of the best known recent critics of Piaget's work is Peter Bryant. His *Perception and Understanding in Young Children* (Methuen, London, 1974) describes a series of careful experiments and a new theory which focuses on the context of children's learning, on the changing frames of reference which they use when making estimates and inferences.
6. *Op. Cit.*, 'Patterns of Growth', p. 21. The earlier quotations are from p. 7 (My italics).
7. *Op. Cit.*, pp. 10, 11.
8. In using 'semiotic' rather than 'articulate' or 'linguistic' I have adopted a term which could cover all sign systems. But 'linguistic' is too narrow and 'articulate' has other special meanings. There may therefore be an element of overlap as the more abstract iconic representatives could be included under 'semiotic' in its broadest connotation. In general, therefore, we may take 'semiotic' as meaning *articulate and language-like*.
9. Professor Bruner is in general agreement with these alterations to his original terminology.
10. Shotter, J., 'Prolegomena to an Understanding of Play', *Journal for the Explanation of Social Behaviour*, Vol. 3, No. 1, p. 82.
11. *Op. Cit.* (Routledge and Kegan Paul, London, 1962).
12. *Science of Education and the Psychology of the Child*, p. 32.
13. *Op. Cit.* (Jossey-Bass, San Francisco, 1974), p. 157.
14. See *Scientific American*, October 1971. T. G. R. Bower, 'The Object in the World of the Infant'.
15. *Op. Cit.*, Chapter 1, 'The Mythology of Deductivism', p. 12.
16. Kohlberg, L., 'From Is to Ought' in Mischel, T. (ed.) *Cognitive Development in Epistemology* (Academic Press, New York, 1971).

CHAPTER 12

A Heuristic Model

We focus upon frontiers; the peak of interest in a symbol tends to occur at the time of revelation, somewhere midway in the passage from the obscure to the obvious. But there is endurance and renewal, too. Discoveries become knowledge only when preserved in accessible form; the trenchant and laden symbol does not become worthless when it becomes familiar, but is incorporated in the base for further exploration. And where there is density in the symbol system, familiarity is never complete and final; another look may always disclose significant new subtleties. Moreover what we read from and learn from a symbol varies with what we bring to it. Not only do we discover the world through our symbols but we understand and reappraise our symbols progressively in the light of our growing experience.

Nelson Goodman[1]

The model that we have built up from Piaget, Bruner and Shotter can be seen as a hierarchy of culturally derived technologies which extend the powers of individuals or groups. In this chapter we will focus more on frontiers and on the exploring individual as he moves through these modes towards what is, to him, shadowy and enigmatic. This involves a consideration of the important but complex question of how art and language are related in education. We cannot, however, deal here with any of the larger problems of aesthetics but will keep our attention, as far as possible, at the level of an exploring child and we will try to develop a model which emphasizes both the child's exploration and his changing attitude to the things which we offer him as instructional aids.

We shall concentrate mainly on the iconic mode and on the transition from it to the semiotic mode. Words and mathematical signs are the main instruments of this most abstract technology of communication. But they, like maps and tools and all the other instruments of human extension at more concrete levels, can be used either externally in action or internally in rational or meditative thought. Even at the interpersonal level we learn to think 'through' someone else, to empathize, as we project ourselves into their shoes.

It will now be apparent that this attempt to understand education as starting, and being essentially concerned, with what is problematic and mysterious leads naturally into the domain of religion. It eliminates 'the problem of R. E.' by relocating it wherever a child has intimations of love and truth and beauty. Many of the world's religions have recognized this and in their varied rites and teachings they have proclaimed that numinous experience can be sought and shared at many levels: at the levels of poetry, art and music; at the active and pre-active interpersonal levels too. Indeed many faiths have had recourse to the same personal pronoun to indicate the profoundly intimate character of Man's response to the universe—that THOU of wonder which is discovered first between a mother and a child and which is then re-invoked in prayer and friendship.

Each instructional level derives from, and involves, the use of those which are less abstract. Nevertheless the model of the four modes of instruction is rather like a four storey house without stairs, in that it assumes differences of level without saying much about how a learner moves, or can be helped to move, upwards or downwards. It was with such problems in mind that it seemed necessary to reserve the word 'symbolic' so that it could be used in reference to the creative use of signs or objects or pictures or actions in the process of exploring meanings at any level. We shall see that such symbolic exploration is often, but not necessarily, of a kind which leads to a move into a mode of greater abstraction. We noted the occasional prophetic functions of parents or teachers who symbolically open the way for subsequent learning. This is part of a process which need not be entirely mysterious and we shall now consider it more closely.

I propose to sketch a model which is complementary to that of the four instructional modes. It may be called the heuristic or frontier model and will be mainly concerned with the exploratory and 'upward' movements of an individual learner as he penetrates the progressively more abstract levels of cultural communication.

We have already seen, in Chapter 8 the main elements of this heuristic model. It is sketched out by an infant when he first crawls away from his mother at the age of about ten months. At this decisive moment a bond is snapped which had, according to Shotter, tied mother and child in psychological sym- biosis and at that moment a new 'educational' relationship is established. With newly acquired autonomy the infant goes off on his own for a brief foray; but he is free only within a very protected space. His toys and other 'transitional objects' are still around. His mother too is there on the perimeter and she herself contributes to the shaping of this new space in which the infant works or plays. There are, however, two kinds of limit to this potential space: firstly those normative ones which are laid down by parents or teachers and which establish social or prudential constraints, a fire-guard for example, bed-time, or an incest taboo. The purpose of such limitations will usually not be clear to the learner, but from our theoretical standpoint such things need to be seen as creating space as well as limiting it. Then there is the child's own heuristic frontier at which he is free to make discoveries and mistakes and to extend his grasp on the world. This is, in an existential sense, *his own* and it cannot be conceptualized in isolation, without an exploring person at its centre.

Here, then, is a diagramatic, that is, iconic version of the child's field of exploration—the first stage of our heuristic model.

104

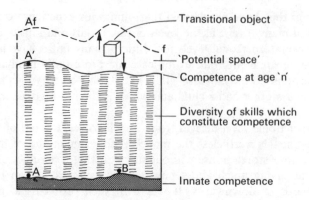

Figure 9. Heuristic model, first stage

In this diagram the two vertical margins represent social and environmental constraints which are not entirely unchangeable, but from the child's view point may appear so. Some questions are begged or by-passed by the shaded base which represents innate competence. Point A might be taken as standing for inherited competence for language, though we can leave for discussion the question of just how much is programmed or open. The child's developed competence A' at the age of, let us say, six years, partly reflects his inherited talents but also the fact that his language ability has been nurtured by experience. This may not be so for other talents. Let us suppose that B represents an innate spatial and visual competence which has not been much enhanced by upbringing. The peak on the dotted frontier line represents this unrealized potential. Here is a sector of competence in a six-year old in which education is likely to bring development. The opportunity to play autonomously with a new and appropriate toy or a new teacher offering suitable challenges might bring about a rapid advance. In one sense all these points are glaringly obvious, for they reflect the hopeful realism of any teacher who has worked with children and known their unpredictable spurts and hesitations. The element of novelty comes from the attempt to fit such learning processes into a conceptual schema in which innate and enhanced competence, play and discovery are all related.

The child's frontier is a resultant both of its own activity, expressing competence, and of its culture. If a six-year old were isolated from all external stimuli and opportunity for action, if for example it were sound asleep, its potential space would be in abeyance, for the frontier which defines such space is a function of intentionality, action and freedom. But such a child would still possess the enhanced competence which it has been acquiring throughout its life. Competence is made up of powers and play in the passive sense; while play, in the active sense, and exploration is its expression.

In any educational or heuristic situation both frontier and potential space are realities, albeit somewhat abstract ones, with which we have to come to terms and we do this either as learners or as teachers. As learners we have a subjective awareness of our own limits, that is of where our problems lie; as teachers we are more objective. The learner experiences his freedom and his frontier in ways in which feeling and symbolic insights predominate. Teachers and parents need to conceptualize such a process empathically, thinking, for example, about what a child is feeling and where *his* problems lie. Inevitably, however, teachers see these things in the wider, more analytic and elaborate frame of their own experiences and expectations. It is to this asymmetry, central to all educational relationships, that we now turn.

THE DYAD

At the heart of every educational process is the basic dyad, parent/child, teacher/learner, master/apprentice. For the sake of simplicity we are leaving on one side the complex and powerful social matrix in which every dyad is lodged. The educational dyad is always more or less hierarchical and more or less asymmetrical, for one person looks up and one looks down, one knows more while feeling less, and one knows less while feeling more. *Si jeunesse savoit; si sagesse pouvoit.* But this is not always a matter of age. A young adult education tutor, for example, may have attained levels of skill and conceptual grasp which give him real authority over a much older student. Once the asymmetry has been overcome, when the apprentice draws level with the master, a partnership is established and another kind of dyad emerges, one that is the elementary unit of all mature, cooperative endeavour. This too, like solitary exploration, will contain learning experiences; but it is not education.

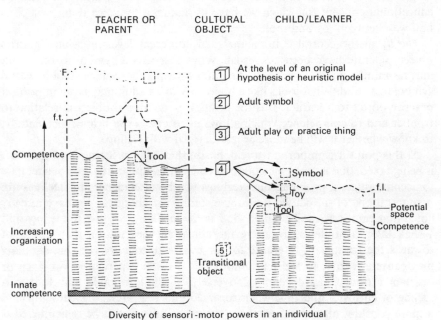

Figure 10. The dyad: heuristic model, second stage

Because the dyad of education is asymmetrical, we need to distinguish both the higher, more extensive viewpoint and the lower, more limited one. In this dyad the two participants are also changing, though at different rates. On the other hand there are many *things* involved in the process which do not change or develop—toys, pictures, or the printed page for example. These relatively constant things may, however, be viewed from startlingly different perspectives. The asymmetrical model which I am proposing (Figure 10) helps to make clear how it is that the same thing or the same sign or even the same action, may generate quite different meanings according to its place in the educational hierarchy. It should be noted that in this diagram F stands for the Frontier of a whole culture, f. t. and f. l. represent the teacher's and learner's frontier.

A number of points can be emphasized in the 3-Frontier model of the educational dyad:

Firstly we need to give some consideration to the relationship between a teacher's frontier and the frontier of his own culture. The authority of a discipline, its key concepts and assumptions which hold together all those who share in its conviviality[2] are created and sustained by researchers or creative people on that frontier and a teacher's attitude to such people will have an important influence on his work.

Secondly for both teacher and learner an educational object has been indicated in the potential space. The vertical arrows suggest how such a play object can be either pushed 'up' towards the frontier as a symbolic probe *or* it can be assimilated, instrumentally, as part of a skill. In the potential space of the child learner there is shown one nameless square which represents an educational concept for which we have no name, a 'practice thing', which is half way between toy and tool.

Thirdly in the central column the many different levels at which cultural objects operate have been suggested. What is a useful symbol to one adult may be mumbo jumbo to another. An adult's weapon or tool may be a powerful symbol to a child. What looks like a 'mere' toy to an adult may be an important practice object to a learner. It is the position of a cultural object in relation to frontier and to competence which allows us to categorise it and, incidentally, to know whether it will be more or less charged with feeling.

At this point it is important to emphasize that when a learner's competence is being taxed, that is when his skills and conceptual apparatus are not adequate to accommodate a problem, then feelings will be in evidence; for feelings are manifestations of unfocused and unconsummated energies. We have already noted that emotions can be understood as the meanings we give to feelings and I shall take 'attitude' as meaning the consistent orientation that we adopt towards the frontier in reference to our own emotions. A very big anomaly may cause a learner to feel fear, and if this is often experienced, a craven or resistant attitude may develop. Conversely, a small anomaly may lead to a feeling of curiosity and this, when repeated and reinforced may develop into a more constant attitude of enquiry. The practical point to be remembered is that when a learner moves up to his frontier, then, though competence tends to wane, feelings will be much in evidence and the things that he works with will be more symbolic in that they increase possible meaning, and less instrumental in that they do not yet increase control, though they may do so later.

We now turn our attention to visual aids and to their function in creating a bridge between enactive and semiotic modes of learning. We shall leave till the next chapter the problems raised by the *intrinsic* value of activities in one or other of the modes, as in dancing (enactive) or painting (iconic) for example.

WHAT DOES A VISUAL AID AID?

The brief answers to this question, and a summary of our theoretical perspective, are as follows:

(i) Visual aids can function as play things.

(ii) They can be objects for practice, establishing graphic and visual skills.

(iii) They can be the basis for exploration of the forms of the visual world (i.e. the practice of fine art). Notice all the above are within the iconic field and, with changes of wording, parallel statements could be made about music and the aural world.

(iv) Visual aids can be used as simulations, offering scope for imaginary explorations into the world of nature and of society. In this they provide a condensed alternative to the real world in which vicarious enactive or interpersonal experience may be sought. They bring a more extensive, concrete world into the classroom.'

(v) Visual aids function as pointers towards the more abstract semiotic mode.

In the last three, though especially in (iii) and (v), the visual aid is a frontier icon.[3] In an art lesson the child may look at some simple device of form or colour and then see *through* it to an imaginative creation of his own. Or in a geography or science lesson, he may be presented with a simulation of the real world in which some problem may be posed; but here the educationist would be right to say 'better, if possible *do* the experiment'. And in the fifth category visual aids can turn the learner towards the more abstract semiotic mode.

The first move—play—is one which a child does with the minimum of encouragement. The teacher's skill in timing and in getting the mood right enables play to develop in any of four 'serious' ways: towards increasing competence (practising graphic skills), towards exploring the iconic world (art), towards exploring the more concrete world of people or nature (actively looking at pictures), or, finally, towards discovering the more abstract world of signs (through diagrams, see Chapter 13).

I propose to illustrate this by a practical example, part of an unsophisticated but effective curriculum unit designed for Sudanese primary schools. The map and the picture (Figures 11 and 12) were designed for children of about 10 or 11 years old. There was a rich source book in Arabic called *Ways of Living in the Sudan* for the teachers, and for the children there were a pair of detailed

108

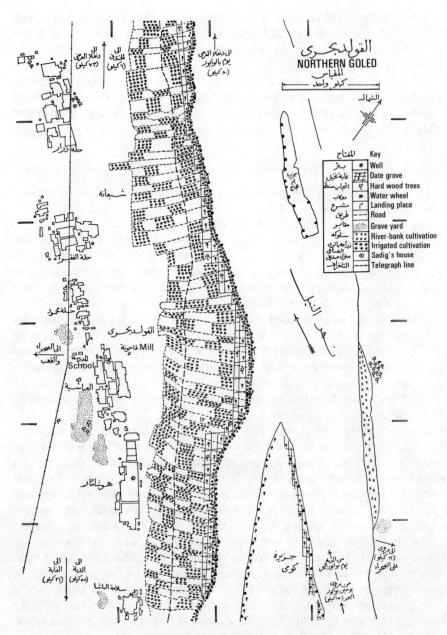

Figure 11. Nile map. (Reproduced from *Ways of Living in the Sudan*, by permission of Publications Bureau, Ministry of Education, Republic of the Sudan)

 المواقف التعليمية (ريف)

Figure 12. Nile picture. (Reproduced from *Ways of Living in the Sudan*, by permission of Publications Bureau, Ministry of Education, Republic of the Sudan)

pictures and a map showing the home area of each of nine 'families' that were studied. As a slightly formal method, suited to large classes and to a poor country, it was very effective, both in building up the teacher's knowledge and in giving the whole class a series of simulations of reality which could be explored. The children were also able to enjoy using a wide range of graphic and cartographic sills—writing stories about the families, learning some of their folk songs and, most important with the more 'primitive' and distant families such as the Azande, they could be encouraged to understand unfamiliar attitudes and customs.

This was my own first encounter with a carefully thought out curriculum package of the kind which is now common in America and Britain. It will be evident that many social and geographical objectives were pursued in this project and many general skills of hand and eye too. Some of these were in the minds of the team who produced the material when they started. Others emerged as time went on.

It may be possible to extract from this simple but successful example of curriculum development some idea of the wide range of functions which pictures can perform in education. This particular picture and map represent the village of Goled on the Northern Nile as it was thirty years ago. A certain amount of background information as to locality and life histories would be given by the teacher but the teaching was slanted to enable the children to learn as much as possible from the pictures and maps. Here in approximate order of difficulty are some of the main activities in which the children might be directly engaged in response to the picture.

> Scanning for recognition
> Scanning for lay-out
> Colouring
> Tracing
> Copying
> Identifying people in the story
> Finding routes
> Imagining hidden things
> Estimating distances
> Drawing things or actions known about but not
>   shown.
> Explaining processes, orally or by diagram,
>   e.g. the water wheel.
> Empathizing into tensions or anxieties—e.g.
>   the long absent son in Egypt.
> Extrapolating into time, e.g. the annual cycle
>   of crops or of the river's flood.
> Looking to the future, e.g. the scope for, and problem of, new
>   farming methods.

Many further refinements of skill and deduction could be followed when the map was used as well. No practising teacher would attempt to grade his teaching of skills in such an exhaustive, systematic way. But the list does suggest how some iconic skills are giving scope for expository and explanatory language use and, further up the scale, for discussion of problems which cannot be fully explained by a diagram but which require understanding of temporal processes and of tensions and uncertainties.

If a picture is intended to provide simulations of real experience it needs to be *rich*—full of detail and possibility. Then, if its explorable, frontier possibilities are to be used to the full, it is usually necessary for a teacher to assist the process. If on the other hand a picture is to be used as an aid to discovery, if it is to be used to assist the move into the semiotic mode, then it will often be stripped of detail and become a skeleton ikon which can easily be manipulated or taken to pieces in the learner's mind—formal operations. Finally, it is worth emphasizing that maps, like many diagrams, though they may apear simpler than pictures, are at a further degree of abstraction from reality. But, they can also be readily enriched by the imaginative work of a viewer. All such skeleton diagrams offer two contrasted possibilities. They can either be clothed—imaginatively, and in this they are often a useful mnemonic, or they can be taken to pieces for greater articulation.[4]

NOTES

1. Nelson Goodman, *The Languages of Art* (O. U. P., 1969).
2. Michael Polanyi uses this word to describe a social context of trust and truth which is prior to, and a condition for, a person's awareness of value. See Chapter VII, 'Conviviality' in *Personal Knowledge*, pp. 203–245 (Routledge & Kegan Paul, London, 1958).
3. The third and fifth moves are indicated by the double arrow in Figure 13 in the next chapter.
4. Information theory expresses this difference in a way which, at first sight, is paradoxical. There is more 'information', using the word in the technical sense, in the map than in the picture because it is tighter, less ambiguous, less problematic than the picture; just as the picture is less problematic than reality. A sign is rich in information by virtue of what it *excludes*. So, other things being equal, language carries more information than either maps or pictures.

CHAPTER 13

Exploration

> An understanding of this matter will be attained rather by our rising above
> the literal sense of words ... For the reader we must even use drawings
> and illustrations, but he must rise above these too.
>
> Nicholas of Cusa[1] (*Of learned ignorance*)

The problem 'What do maps do?' is a particular version of a more general
educational question which has been bothering us: how does this object, this
word or phrase, in this or that context, facilitate a learner's acquisition of more
abstract representations of structure? How does a child break through from
one mode to the next? In this chapter I shall argue that this is a frontier phenomenon but in order to understand it we have to distinguish between pure
exploration (e.g. art for art's sake) and that kind of exploration which leads to
discoveries or the uncovering of structure. It is the latter, much more than the
former, which is characteristic of successful education.

I first came upon the map problem at Abbotsholme where I worked for twelve
years. This sometimes involved teaching geography to small groups of Sixth
Formers. Abbotsholme was a school, founded in 1889, with splendid ideas
about an education of hand and heart, eye and brain. Anyone teaching there
who even partly understood the intuitions of the founder, Cecil Reddie, could
not fail to recognize that the educational process was going on at many different
levels. It was clear that music and art, mathematics and rock-climbing, science
and worship, could all be part of one process in which a whole community
was learning. But it must be admitted that we often jibbed and compromised
and failed to realize fine possibilities. With my geography group we would try
to achieve real education for three or four terms and then, gradually, we would
settle down to the 'A' level syllabus. This is not to suggest, however, that either
syllabusses or such compromises should be despised.

James was one of a group of five geographers. He had failed his eleven-plus
and came to us from a suburban home. His parents kept a sports shop somewhere in the Midlands. James was keen on Rugby and running, on Scouts and
on many other activities. His academic work was exceptionally neat. But there
was a spectacular snag. He could not write articulate grammatical sentences
or paragraphs. His essays looked beautiful—neat title, margins and what
looked like paragraphs—until you actually started reading. The syntax was
all at sea, the phrasing was inconsequential and there was no apparent plan.
James had obtained two good 'O' levels, in art and woodwork and he had

scraped through in his best subjects—geography and biology. He eventually passed English language after failing four times. He was an extreme example of a problem which is common enough in schools once you leave the ranks of the articulate convergers—the problem of how to start arranging 'your own ideas' in a logical sequence. It is a much harder task than most educated adults realize. Connected with this difficulty is the idea, which many students have, that there is one best, logical way of developing a line of argument. This may be so but once the student realizes that there are usually a large number of possible ways and that one of these may suit him better than it would suit a lawyer, he has surmounted an important hurdle. Usually the train of ideas can be assembled from the marshalling yard in many different ways. The great thing is to start shunting.

James' own break-through was to do with a railway line and it came only six months before 'A' levels. A weekend essay had to be written on the economic geography of East Africa and I suggested, grasping at a straw, that he might plan his essay as a map of the Kenya-Uganda railway and chop it into six sections, on each of which he could write a paragraph. The trick worked and an articulate essay was produced. This device only succeeded because that particular railway system *is* itself a single line with very few branches. Nevertheless this map at this particular moment offered James a much needed template for a logical written discourse.

It would be wrong to leave this particular example without pointing to the importance of an extensive field of activity in which the break-through happened. Because James was keeping up successful pressure on many fronts, like Clausewitz, he was able to wait for a favourable moment to break through at this critical point. But the military metaphor is not quite adequate. Competence and its exercise create or make available supplies of energy which would otherwise not be tapped. And again it is not a question of breaking through *anywhere* for James. For him and for many others like him, articulate expression in language or in mathematics is a *sine qua non* for further development. Without such facility these students are cut off from mastery of the most flexible and the most generative technologies of thought.

Two questions now become apparent:

(i) Though there may be a psychological connection between successes in, for example, running (enactive) or in friendship (interpersonal) and the break-through to the articulate mode, and though from the existential view-point these may all be frontier experiences, *is* there a fundamental difference between pushing out at what you are 'good at' and breaking through to what you feel 'bad at'? The difference between these, between exploring and discovering, and the importance of both is examined in the next section.

(ii) Are there certain kinds of diagram or visual aid which are particularly conducive to the transformation from iconic to articulate skills. [7]

(James, by the way, who is only thinly disguised, *did* get his 'A' levels and became an enterprising teacher.)

EXPLORING AND DISCOVERING

If we are to understand better the problem of what the map did for James it is necessary to make a brief digression and to clarify the difference between exploration and discovery. Exploration can, in principle, go on indefinitely, without result. But discovery is an event, one which involves the uncovering of some structural relationship that was not evident before.[2] As we have seen in Chapters 9 and 10, if we postulate a structure we are also assuming that we, or someone else, has already identified a system within which structural relations could be usefully investigated. This is a larger scale version of the situation we encountered in Chapter 2 with Sarah and her word shapes. Questions of great moment may remain in a person's mind as a powerful but unclear symbol for a long time. The formulation of a question and the act of discovery are each the culmination of a growing sense of pattern.

Consider the exploration of America. Columbus sailed westwards for seventy days—exploring. Most of his crew were difficult to discipline. Whether or not they really thought they would fall off the edge of the world, it is impossible to know. But Columbus and a few friends had a special kind of knowledge which kept them going. Then one morning land was discovered. Columbus sailed on, encircled that bit of land and so 'discovered an island'. The voyage of exploration was performed mainly in what we would call 'the enactive mode', but Columbus' discovery of *coast* put an iconic limit on seventy days of ocean. He then made a further move when he called the island 'one of the Indies'. This naming is a first step up the scale of abstraction, out of the iconic and into the articulate mode, and the fact that Columbus happened to be wrong makes no difference. What made naming possible was that he and his more cultured companions had a rough, spherical world map in which they located their island. It would be reasonable to doubt whether without such a mental image they could have successfully endured seventy days in an empty ocean with a complaining crew.

It would therefore be correct, in these terms, to say that the Amer-Indian tribes explored the Americas as they penetrated from the north, but not, in normal usage, to say that they discovered the continent. The discovery of Vinland by the Norsemen is a nice marginal case and their claim to have discovered America rests not so much on whether they reached its shores, which most people concede, but on the degree to which their discoveries were communicated and assimilated to the map consciousness of other Europeans. Hence the alleged significance of the famous Vinland map forgery. It appeared to alter the context of the Norse explorations. A similar analysis could be made in terms of China or any other extensive civilization with accumulated geographical records. Discoveries *transform* explorations into more abstract and communicable modes and their acceptability depends partly on the framework into which they are fitted.

Just as the explorer will often press on to the limits when the prospects of discovery are meagre, so the artist or musician or poet will use skill and vision to extend the domain where he is most competent. He will make works of art which *are*, or at least which reflect, his explorations. But few artists are concerned to explain what they are doing. They do not often make *discoveries*. Scientists on the other hand are committed both to exploring the world and to transforming their findings into an almost world-wide, articulate domain. So, though the actual findings of scientists are mainly in what we should describe as the enactive domain and though their explanations often start at the iconic level of model-making, their discoveries are legitimated at the semiotic level where they can be expressed in words and mathematics and then communicated, tested, falsified or revised by others in the community of science.[3]

The roles of explorer–artist, explorer–scientist and teacher often overlap but their essential tasks are different and can be summarized as follows:

> *An explorer–artist* pushes back the Frontier and produces works in a chosen section of his particular mode, e.g. abstract painting in the iconic mode. Rather similar in the enactive mode is the explorer–climber or the speliologist; but here the work is action not making.
>
> *The explorer–scientist* investigates the structure of a substance or the behaviour pattern of an animal species and then transforms that concrete pattern up the scale—to map, to mathematics, to 'law'. He discovers or abstracts the pattern and makes it as communicable, as refutable and as manipulable as possible. *The teacher*, by contrast, is interested in downward transformations, that is in making knowledge more concrete and more communicable to learners. The scientist makes a theory out of a model, for his peers; the teacher makes a model out of a theory, for his pupils.

AIDS TO TRANSFORMATION

This formulation of the teacher's function may be obvious but it is necessary if we are to clarify the nature of teaching aids in general and of iconic aids in particular. We can now see that certain key diagrams, which I call skeleton ones, may be of particular value in helping a learner to transform his iconic perceptions into articulate ones. The skeleton cube, for instance, ⌗ can be seen *into*, mentally demolished, and reassembled in the mind's eye much more readily than a solid block.[4] It becomes an easy move from this skeleton to $x \times x \times x$. Similarly the map of an unusually simple railway offered James the framework needed to create, for the first time, one of those artificial, articulated constructions that we call an essay.

Some of Tony Buzan's television programmes on how people can improve thinking and learning skills are relevant here.[5] He believes that we should be taught, much more consciously, how to set about assimilating and fostering new ideas. He suggests, for example, that instead of taking wordy notes of lectures we should jot down a few key words around an iconically structured thought diagram. These are similar to my skeleton icons but, by having so

116

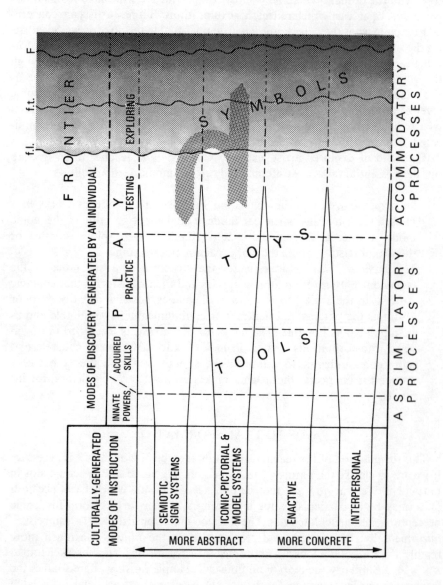

Figure 13. A composite model

much verbiage in a non-linear form, they leave open many problems—in the marshalling yard as it were—until the last moment.[6] The effect of such systems is to make a student more confident in moving to and fro across the gap between iconic representation and articulate language. In this field there is much research to be done, which could produce great improvements in the creaking teaching methods with which most teachers are cumbered; cumbered, not because the methods are respected, but because there is so little that is manifestly better.

In thinking about these problems of how we cross from one mode to another, how the learner's unknown is often the teacher's known and how the mastery of the various modes of instruction is cumulative, I attempted to integrate both the diagrams in the form of one matrix which relates the two models we have been using—that of the four culturally derived modes of instruction and the competence–play–frontier model (Figure 13). I find this composite chart an interesting aid to thought, as it sets out all the possible variations of the basic educational dyad and one can locate in it either the most primitive and concrete interactions of teacher and learner or the most exalted ones. Essentially the three central columns refer to the learning field or potential space in which all education takes place, mechanical practice for skills on the left and probing of shadowy frontiers on the right. The boat-hook construction illustrates one example of the alternatives which face an explorer—to press on or to structure and transform newly acquired data. Along this curving bridge of transformation from exploration in one mode to discovery of structure in another, our particular iconic problem in this chapter and a number of other similar educational problems, can be opened up and analysed. The branching hook in the diagram should be regarded as moveable, for at different levels it can indicate the nature of the choice between exploration (e.g. 'art for art's sake') and discovery (transformation to a more abstract mode).

The sequence: play, testing, exploring over the frontier, discovery, playing with new structural elements, practice, competence, can now be seen as offering the main constituents of that bridge across the gap with which we started in Chapter 8. 'What goes across?' we asked. The answer was 'Structure goes one way and questions go the other'. The theoretical route by which we have attempted to explore this gap may or may not be fruitful for research and for further exploration; but the gap is real and so are the difficulties with which it confronts us.

NOTES

1. Quoted in Santillana (ed.) *The Age of Adventure* (Mentor Books).
2. This is the distinction which Ryle draws between task words and achievement words in *The Concept of Mind*, p. 150. But he does not follow up the implications of saying 'In applying an achievement word we are asserting that some state of affairs obtains over and above that which consists in performance ... of the subservient task activity'. It is this 'over and above' context that we are interested in.
3. There are a number of ideas here which relate to Popper's thought including his concept of a Third World or universe of objective knowledge. But I do not think his analysis copes with the enormously important world of feeling, the shadowy approaches, to

the 'Third World'. See his 'Epistemology Without a Knowing Subject' in *Objective Knowledge*, pp. 106–152 (O. U. P., 1971).

4. In psychological terms this relates to the move from concrete operations to formal operations (Piaget). It is best to retain our terms, semiotic, iconic, etc. for the technologies and processes of communication and instruction which are, closely intertwined.

5. Buzan, A. *Use Your Head*, B. B. C. publications, 1973.

6. Yates, Frances, *The Art of Memory* (Routledge and Kegan Paul, London, 1966, also in Penguin Books) on classical and pre-print 'memory theatres' is also of great interest. These theatres were mental constructions—mnemonic aids to rhetoric—of great complexity.

CHAPTER 14

Personal Knowledge

We shall not cease from exploration
And the end of all our exploring
Will be to arrive where we started
And know the place for the first time.
Through the unknown, remembered gate
When the last of earth left to discover
Is that which was the beginning;
At the source of the longest river
The voice of the hidden waterfall
And the children in the apple tree
Not known, because not looked for
But heard, half-heard, in the stillness
Between the waves of the sea.

T. S. Eliot, *Little Gidding*.

In this book we have been turning knowledge back to front, trying to see it as that which is struggled for, rather than as that which is possessed, as inter- mittent creation rather than as constant facts. Doubtless we need to think of it in both ways, but the perspective of education should be more concerned with process than with attainment. We must 'focus upon frontiers' for it is there that new concepts first become apprehensible and the dynamic of such 'prehension'[1] as Whitehead called it, is what theory should elucidate.

All knowledge is personal and it may not have escaped the reader's notice that the image of the frontier which is central to this book has itself a personal history. One cannot be addicted to mountain climbing, as I have been for many years, without often being tugged by frontiers. This enactive frontier experience came first for me and was powerfully charged with feeling; but as an iconic diagram it soon began to fit phenomena other than mountains. The advancing or retreating edges of a system—whether cloud or amoeba, flame or tide, or the groping enquiries of a child—offer more than aesthetic interest. One comes to reflect on the nature of the system which supports and pushes out the frontier edge. What are the internal structures and information processes which sustain the advance of the flame or the living system, and how are they re-ordered in times of retreat or slack? Have you noticed the violence with which a soft white margin of cloud grips and shakes the wing tip of an aircraft? And what of the subtle time–space boundary which surrounds a school community, that line at which manners are prone to change and rules are stretched and broken? Or, less subtle and sometimes tinged with farce, what of the semi-permeable membrane with which the staff of a school wrap themselves round? It is with this that they preserve the special mores of the group within the staff room or prescribe the pattern of encounter in the corridors so that, here too, form and face may be maintained. What kind of information is generated at such boundaries in your school and is it mediated with humanity or belligerence? All these group interfaces display one thing in common: we mark them with ritual and with symbolic acts. It is easy to be sentimental about smiles and to reduce raised eyebrows to a joke, but they are part of the fundamental currency of group interaction. They are not mere tokens but transforming acts which control the flow of information in a system. But here we are moving into areas of educational sociology which are only now being opened up. Our focus so far has been mainly on one particular kind of boundary, the existential frontier of the learning child, and on the asymmetry between this and the way the teacher construes his own world.

FRONTIER ALTERNATIVES

Most of us recall some moments of creation in our adult life, some small work of research or art, where at least we felt a breath of exposure to the unknown. But as teachers, our creative work is concerned, not with our culture's frontier, not with our own, but with the child's frontier. All education starts at that point, with intuition, empathy and guesswork. There are two possible developments when the frontier is reached.

The teacher may use his power of simplifying and his imagination to create a situation, a curricular experience, in which structure is discoverable. The learner perceives the situation first as a difficulty, next as a problem and then breaks into it, transforming it to a more abstract mode (i.e. making a discovery). Then he plays with it in a way which involves more and more practice and control until the new concept or skill is assimilated; or, as we have seen, the problem may be too big for him and it will remain wholly or partly enigmatic, held for him as a persistent symbol. He can still work at this problem area as an artist might, weaving his poems or his patterns in its penumbra. Such work may generate a sense of pleasure and of intrinsic worth. But should education be interested in the other route—towards articulate expression? If personal exploration and creation is important, and if the different modes of instruction are all in their way, good, is there any special virtue in pushing education towards the more abstract mode? Or in more general terms: need artists be articulate outside their medium? I think the answer should be 'yes'; there *is* virtue in articulateness, for everyone, and the reason is that no man is, except for short periods, an island.

In the previous chapter we differentiated between exploration and discovery. In so doing we underlined a difficulty which relates both to the theoretical model (Figure 12 above) and to an important curriculum question about 'doing your own thing'. The theoretical problem is this: why do we need to speak as though exploration by a child of his own frontier interest (say athletics) is similar to his attempts to penetrate a more abstract mode of representation? One suggestion was that when psychological or 'motivational' energies are generated they affect the whole frontier; success anywhere eventually helps everywhere. This may be so but there is more to it than this. When a learner moves out to a frontier situation he is emotionally exposed and his competence of skill and of knowledge is fully stretched. We noted that in this situation feelings are of great importance and are also likely to be contagious; this is one reason for a teacher being available, for then his own values may be perceived and if seen to be appropriate they may be acquired with no word spoken.

There is a further point. In frontier situations we are more ready to 'think laterally', to improvise and to draw on all our experience. We try new models, look round them, toy with them and ask for help. Movement up and down the known modes comes more readily when we are grappling with difficulties. And further, the learner's unknown ground is often the teacher's known ground which gives him the knowledge and occasion to help. It is for these three reasons: motivation, feeling, and modal mobility that we can locate exploration and the acquisition of mastery of more abstract modes in the frontier zone. It is here that we learn to interpret and control feeling and so to develop moral attitudes. In frontier situations teachers play a crucial part, they help to create the situation and they help to sustain and monitor it.

A CENTRAL QUESTION FOR SECONDARY EDUCATION: DOING ONE'S OWN THING?

In relatively affluent countries secondary education is being conceived of less as the training of children from culturally favoured homes or of bright children for élite roles and more as a universal preparation for ... something. Critics of the system sometimes claim that the whole school-based organization of post-primary education should be dissolved or drastically changed. Whether or not this minority are right, a larger number of critics could be found who would advocate wholesale changes in the methods of secondary and tertiary education.

For the sake of argument, however, let us make an assumption about this matter: that secondary education in thirty to fifty years time will be envisaged largely in terms of groups of young people learning and being taught to do demanding, useful and creative things, things which are worthwhile in themselves; at the same time secondary education will become less concerned with preparation for specific jobs or with the objective that young people can 'take their place in society'. In short, we shall assume that secondary education will become frontier-oriented rather than fact-oriented. This assumes that training in basic skills of many kinds should dominate education up to the age of about 12 and that culture and creativity could increasingly dominate it afterwards. Economic and utilitarian considerations will continue to operate but they must be seen as constraints on the system and not as giving it direction or power.

The general argument of this book points in the direction of such an open, exploratory education, which will draw on the essentially questing, questioning, socially enterprising nature of young human beings. So it is worth adding, that whether we live in a poor country or in a so-called advanced one, only an education conceived of as being energized by the learners themselves is likely to be economically possible in the less affluent and less expansive century which lies ahead.

This leads to our curricular problem. Why should not young artists paint, young musicians play and young climbers climb out to their limits; and everyone else at school or university be encouraged to follow their exploratory inclinations on their own frontiers? If we are not going to rely on utilitarian or economic arguments what is the educational case against such claims? There is, I believe, a powerful one. It can be put baldly in this form: an illiterate artist can scarcely be called an artist any more than Columbus could have properly been called an explorer if he had had no mental map. In pre-literate societies there have, no doubt, been great artists, but they were not people who pursued an individualistic enthusiasm; they spoke for, and were immersed in, the traditions and acts of a group. They were closely knit to others and to traditions by words, symbols, rituals and shared memories. One can, perhaps, explore without a mentor and without a culture; but to develop meaning you need others and to make discoveries you need a context. So in terms of our modern curriculum problem it is not merely the energy and the skill to carry someone out to a frontier that counts; it is also the complementary capacity to use, and move among, the several modes of representation.

James' problem as he approched 'A' levels, about how to articulate the knowledge that he had, is common enough and one which most children need help to solve. It is crucial. Without positive mastery of abstract modes of thought a person's performance in any of them will be impoverished. To be articulate is to be like the hand, jointed, not too heavily programmed and with a wide span.

There are complementary problems which are nearly as acute. How can we help convergent, 'well motivated', academically promising, students, especially if they are teachers under training, to remain free or to recover mobility so that they too can act and feel and think in many modes, including the primary, wordless encounters of the interpersonal domian?

PEOPLE

One of the results of a theory of education emphasizing the transferability of knowledge is that it highlights the importance of the educational system and diminishes the importance of people. Yet people, characterized by a capacity to alter and create patterns and to do unexpected things, are the essential components of that generative system which is called human culture. Education is drawing people into that culture—yes, initiating them; but not so that they arrive as the educated ones; rather that they become discoverers and creators of what was not there before.

People, and perhaps especially teachers, cannot stop learning; or if they do they become sad or ill or boring. There is one respect in which teachers differ from other learned professions, such as doctors or lawyers. The main aim of a lawyer or a doctor is normative. There exist professionally and socially defined levels of health or of social harmony which are sometimes hard to reach, but such norms do constitute the level at which a medical or legal task is known to be completed. With teachers, and especially with secondary teachers, our aim is to ensure health or basic harmony *in order* that the professionally interesting work may start. If ever a teacher should encounter a normal child one of his first tasks might be to help it to become different. Our norms are starting points.

This is a romantic view of the teaching profession—important, yet only half the truth. Despite our interest in diversity we *are* tied together by shared standards. But how are these generated and sustained if they are not written in some code of ethics? The answer, again, is to do with frontiers. When men have to deal with acute social crises or unprecedented moral problems these are marked by symbols of a strongly personal kind. At one level these may be embedded in highly charged and ambiguous utterances—the words of a demagogue for example. Or again the symbols which enable us to sustain and transform stress and doubt may be of a religious kind—acts or objects which point to personal renewal—the ritual by the cattle camps, those vows we spoke, the icon of suffering borne. Here again the symbol will generally, in some form or another, be a person or of a personal kind. It need not be a political saviour like Marx or Mao, though these are certainly potent as focuses of hope and change. Nor need it be a cosmic, spiritual redeemer, a Christ or Avatar. Smaller figures serve their turn, but they all provide the background for the judgements we make about the value or direction of what we do.

The Communion of Saints is one of the more tractable Christian doctrines. We do not, as some philosophers maintain, reason our way through moral conflicts as lonely stoics; nor do we often hurl ourselves, solitary, into the Sartrean abyss. Certainly we exercise our rational powers, draw on our stock of courage and seek advice, but we also invoke what Bruner calls our 'competence models', those men and women who showed us the way and imprinted their standards on us. There can be few teachers who are not aware of such mentors at their elbow during moments of crisis. Sometimes they upbraid or cheer us as they did long ago; at other times we just remember them and their work.

NOTE

1. A. N. Whitehead's term. 'We feel what is there and transform it to what is here'. Victor Lowe, *Understanding Whitehead*, p. 40 (Johns Hopkins, Baltimore, 1962).

APPENDIX

Man: a Course of Study

The outline below will make most sense to a reader who is familiar with the mass of curriculum material comprising the M. A. C. O. S. package. But a similar approach can be taken with much cheaper and simpler materials. The point which the table makes is that conceptual structures and an awareness of resources, of children's skills and interests and of teachers' capacities, rather than an impressive list of learning objectives should be the starting point of most curricular reform.

Conceptual Themes	Data Sources	Classroom Techniques	Learning Methods
Life cycle (including reproduction)	1. *Primary Sources*	*Examples*	Inquiry, investigation (problem-defining, hypothesizing, experimentation, observation, interviewing, literature searching, summarizing and reporting)
Adaption	Student experiences Behaviour of family Behaviour of young children in school Behaviour of animals	Individual and group research, e.g. direct observation or reading of texts	
Learning			
Aggression		Large and small group discussion	
Organization of groups (including group relationships, the family and community, division of labor)	2. *Secondary Sources* Films and slides of animals and Eskimos Recording of animal sounds	Games Role play	Sharing and evaluating of interpretation Accumulating and retaining information

Technology	Recordings of Eskimo myths, legends and poetry	Large and small group projects such as art and construction projects	Exchange of opinion, defence of opinion Exploration of individual feelings
Communication and language	Anthropological field notes		
World view	Written data on humans, other animals and environments	Writing of songs and poems	Exposure to diverse aesthetic styles
Values			

Reproduced with permission from: *Man: A Course of Study*—Curiosity, Competence, Community. J. S. Bruner.

Index